HEAVEN is HERE

Be the Change the World Longs For

TOBIAS STOCKLER

Remnant
Publications
Coldwater MI 49036

Heaven Is Here! Be the Change the World Longs For
By Tobias Stockler

Unless otherwise noted, all Scripture quotations
are taken from the King James Version.

Scripture marked NKJV or *New King James Version* is taken from the
New King James Version®. Copyright © 1982 by Thomas
Nelson, Inc. Used by permission. All rights reserved.

Scripture marked *The Message* is taken from
The Message. Copyright © 1993, 1994, 1995, 1996, 2000, 2001,
2002. Used by permission of NavPress Publishing Group.

Scripture marked *J. B. Phillips New Testament* is taken from
The New Testament in Modern English, J. B. Phillips,
1962 edition, published by HarperCollins.

Scripture marked *Weymouth New Testament* is from
The Weymouth New Testament in Modern Speech.

Scripture marked *Wycliffe Bible* is from The Wycliffe Bible.

Scripture marked RSV is from the Revised Standard Version of the
Bible, copyright © 1946, 1952, and 1971 the Division of Christian
Education of the National Council of the Churches of Christ in the
United States of America. Used by permission. All rights reserved.

Cover design by David Berthiaume
Text Design by Greg Solie • Altamont Graphics

ISBN 978-1-629130-42-2
RP# RP1107

**To contact the author or schedule him to speak, go to
www.heavenisherebook.org**

TABLE OF CONTENTS

GRATITUDE

I would be lying if I left you with the impression that I am smart enough to figure out this entire subject on my own. I am not. Life has often taught me firsthand how little smartness I really have. In this book, I share only what I found out from others; old ideas in fresh words. I am indebted to many great thinkers and communicators, both past and present, for whatever I have said here. I am also indebted to the many humble and quiet people whom I have met along life's journey. It is impossible to trace every thought back to the experience or the person who originated it. Nevertheless, I am grateful to each one who has sparked an idea or matured a thought for me. The greatest contributor to my thinking on this subject of heaven is Jesus Himself. My greatest gratitude is to Him.

FOREWORD

S o you're curious. You've heard of heaven. You have your own ideas about it. Just about all of us do. Our ideas of heaven usually tell us more about ourselves than they do about any actual place. About the only thing most people agree on about heaven is that it is better than what we are experiencing here, which is why almost everyone agrees that *heaven isn't here*.

There are a few other things about heaven that we can probably agree on very quickly. Heaven doesn't have cruelty. It doesn't have injustice or discomfort. We do not know why we agree on these things, though. Science cannot prove any one of those simple statements. Science has no test tube labeled "heaven." No one can grow heaven in a culture in a laboratory. We cannot find it hidden in a rainforest, catch it, and take it back home in a cage. Heaven is hard to study. Most of us want heaven to exist. Many of us are certain it exists. Yet we seem to have no proof.

Our world has changed. Two hundred years ago, a few million white people living in Europe and North America knew heaven was in the future. They were certain heaven was where some people went after they died. They believed this to be real even though they had no access to space travel, knew a lot less about astronomy, and knew nothing about most of the rest of the planet.

Now we have actual photographs and videos and firsthand reports of the marvels of our planet from all over the world, and we have learned a lot about astronomy. We even have people who have been to space and back and can tell us about looking back at our "precious little ball."

Travel and communication have also made the world a lot smaller. I have friends on every continent but Antarctica. We talk to each other. I have learned to appreciate other cultures, other places, other people, and their way of thinking. I would be forced to pay attention to these other cultures and ways of thinking even if I didn't want to.

In our old world, many of us did not like strangers. Rudyard Kipling complained that he did not understand the thinking of people who were different than himself. Kipling described his own experience with the Indian people during his time in their Asian country in his poem "The Stranger."

The Stranger within my gate,
He may be true or kind,
But he does not talk my talk—
I cannot feel his mind.
I see the face and the eyes and the mouth,
But not the soul behind.

The men of my own stock,
They may do ill or well,
But they tell the lies I am wanted to,
They are used to the lies I tell;
And we do not need interpreters
When we go to buy or sell.

The Stranger within my gates,
He may be evil or good,
But I cannot tell what powers control—
What reasons sway his mood;
Nor when the Gods of his far-off land
Shall repossess his blood.

The men of my own stock,
Bitter bad they may be,
But, at least, they hear the things I hear,
And see the things I see;
And whatever I think of them and their likes
They think of the likes of me.

The inability to appreciate those who are different led Kipling to vote in favor of isolation from strangers. Thus, he concluded his poem:

This was my father's belief
And this is also mine:
Let the corn be all one sheaf—
And the grapes be all one vine,
Ere our children's teeth are set on edge
By bitter bread and wine. [1]

Today our world has become so interconnected that we must *like* strangers. We must even cherish them, *all* of them.

In America we learned this the hard way. The United States welcomed all sorts of immigrants. It affirmed in its Declaration of Independence that "all men are created equal," but it did not always treat American Indians well. For our first century, the Native Americans were not legally "people." American Indians were not supposed to become part of our culture. They were strangers.

A trial in April 1879 in Omaha, Nebraska, changed that forever. A few Ponca Indians were arrested and being taken back to live in Oklahoma against their will. Standing Bear, chief of the Ponca Tribe, stood in court to explain why he should be allowed to become part of the American culture that was spreading into his native Nebraska instead of being forced to move to a strange place. His opening words appealed to the judge to be accepted as just another human.

Half facing the audience [Standing Bear], held out his right hand, and stood motionless so long that the stillness of death which had settled down on the audience became almost unbearable. At last, looking up at the judge, he said:

"That hand is not the color of yours, but if I prick it, the blood will flow, and I shall feel pain. The blood is of the same color as yours." [2]

Judge Dundy took the chief's words seriously and decided that Indians were people, and as people, they were free to live as they chose in the United States. It was the first time in history that a US Court acknowledged an Indian as a "person."

Every person on this planet can say the same thing as Standing Bear. Our hands are not all the same color, "but if I prick it, the blood will flow, and I will feel pain. The blood is of the same color as yours." We share a common rock to live on, a common need for life to be valued and nurtured.

This leads us to another truth. As long as one person with blood the same color as mine is being hurt, heaven isn't here. We humans do not have to all think the same thing. We do not have to do the same thing. We do not have to agree with each other. Still, every person must be safe, comfortable, and able to find fulfillment.

I wish there was a "heaven" switch that would suddenly produce safety, comfort, and the opportunity for fulfillment for every person. I wish a magic wand could do the trick. There is no such thing. There is no instant mix just waiting for us to add water and stir. Heaven doesn't appear when charming little girls kiss frogs. Heaven can only come as we change as humans, for human behavior, collectively, is the greatest cause of hell on earth. This hell can be removed as we find a way to change our human behavior, one heart and one individual at a time.

We don't have heaven here and now. The troubles that are in this world lead us to doubt the existence of heaven or to decide it is overrated. These troubles lead us to believe strongly that heaven is somewhere other than this world and some other time than right now. How is *heaven really here?*

Like many of you, I like things that are here and now. I like things that I can experience. I like things that my friends have experienced.

I want a heaven that I can experience here and now. I think that I have found heaven. Whether that is true or not is open to investigation. In the pages of this book, you will be the judge. I invite you to be open-minded and consider all the evidence I've offered. Enjoy hearing me out. In the end, please make up your own mind.

Chapter 1
THE PROBLEM IS FINDING HEAVEN

Our Search

Mount Everest may be just about as close as earth gets to heaven. Its majesty, mystery, tranquility, beauty, and serenity are the stuff of glory. The tremendous achievement of climbing is part of its great allure. If only that were all there was to Everest. The top of the world is no place to stay. When Edmund Hillary and Tenzing Norgay reached the summit on May 29, 1953 for the first time in recorded human history, they stayed all of *fifteen minutes.*

Their brief moment of success hardly did justice to the preparation it required. Fifty years were necessary to find the mountain—fifty years involving thousands of man hours; long marches through India and its neighbors; encounters with tigers, snakes, and malaria; and endless mathematical calculations without a computer. Another hundred years were necessary to develop political relationships and mountaineering to the point where summiting was possible—one hundred years of negotiations and political calculations; of developing equipment and techniques and raising millions of British pounds in funding. Along the way, in mapping and mountaineering, people sacrificed their fortunes and even their lives to the project. One hundred and fifty years of effort and agony to achieve the doorstep of paradise, and the two men stayed for fifteen minutes: one minute for every decade of work!

One hundred mile-an-hour winds at -40 degrees Fahrenheit with low oxygen levels do not make for an ideal destination even if climbing through them to the top of Mount Everest is an achievement. Reaching the goal does not mean you can thrive when you arrive. Mount Everest may be just about as close as earth gets to heaven. But trying to live there is suicide. Each of the hundreds of people to reach the pinnacle of the world intends to go back down and to do it quickly.

It isn't any safer once we get closer to the core of the earth. On January 23, 1960, Lt. Don Walsh of the US Navy and Jacques Piccard spent less than twenty minutes looking around at the bottom of the ocean. The exploration may have been enchanting, but twenty minutes of that reality was all they could risk.[3] Fifty-two years later, James Cameron could only spend about three hours nearly seven miles below the surface of the ocean. [4] Both trips were a very short experience for the time and expense it took to get there.

From the high point of planet earth to its low point, there is lot to attract us. In the more than twelve miles of elevation difference between the top of Everest and the depth of the Challenger Deep of the Mariana Trench, [5] there really is a lot that reminds us of heaven. We've found breathtaking geography and enchanting weather. Most of us have family and friends. We've grown and prepared delicious food and produced delightful music and art. But none of these alone is paradise. We all know from first-hand experience that heaven isn't *here*. Nowhere on earth is completely perfect, offering the opportunity to live, laugh, grow older (no one really wants to actually grow old), and prosper without any danger or heartache.

Our greatest glory is haunted by the dark side of life on earth. In beauty and pleasure, there is danger and treachery. From the bustle of the largest cities to the solitude of the kingdom of the penguins in Antarctica, we have searched the world over for heaven. We have found the most beautiful tropical islands only to see them devastated by a hurricane. We have found glorious caves only to find human skeletons in them. We have cultivated the richest soil only to have a drought destroy our crops. In all the variety, there is one truth that remains certain: our world is a glorious brew of triumphant experience sabotaged by danger and heartache. We are surrounded by joy and difficulty, beauty and challenge, in every place across our globe.

The danger can be controlled sometimes. It is often limited, or humanity could not survive. The difficulties are overcome. These blots in an otherwise glorious and amazing planet are hard. But life is not impossible. We have found ways to cope with it all. Still, our minds ask, *Does it really have to be like this? Couldn't we have a world where perfection is permanent, a planet where we could climb to the top of Everest and stay there as long as we wanted? Couldn't we live anywhere we wanted on our planet and be in paradise? Why do we have to always tolerate the mixed bag of planetary existence? Why put up with an imperfect globe? Why can't we live in heaven right here and right now?*

Can We Build It?

Maybe we should stop looking for paradise and build the perfect reality instead. Humanity certainly has tried. We've built amazing cities with long bridges and tall buildings. We've designed gorgeous parks and intriguing streets. We've built huge international businesses to provide goods and services of all kinds. We have designed governments to protect us. Our accomplishments dazzle us. We wonder at and admire what we have done. Yet for all of our marvelous achievement and hard work, we still don't have heaven. Just ask law enforcement.

Some of us have tried very, very hard to build a nation of heaven. Adolf Hitler was one of many. He organized his nation into a society that benefited millions of people. Inventions out of World War II era Germany make our lives easier to this very day. Back then, thought, sweat, technology, and cooperation fostered great accomplishment. Still, the name Hitler doesn't remind us of heaven. His method of getting heaven included creating hell for millions of other people. He wasn't willing to share his "heaven" with those who were Jewish or who were critical of the Third Reich. In fact, Germany's intellectual strength, educational height, and industrial prowess didn't keep that country's leadership from the worst acts of barbarism.

Iosif Vissarionovich (Joseph) Stalin was another individual who tried to turn his country into heaven. He didn't succeed either. He ordered millions of people to be killed, and they didn't find Stalin's Russia to be heaven at all.

Thousands of other people over hundreds of years have tried to create heaven on earth, and every one of them has failed. They have spent millions of dollars and millions of man hours trying. Human genius and effort have done their best, but we humans have never created Utopia at any point in time.

Our hard work and intelligence have tested every boundary and surpassed every limit. We have worked hard. We have succeeded in amazing endeavors. We can explore anywhere and discover anything. We can tame and use our world. From nuclear science to mechanical science, we can achieve it. From Everest to the Mariana Trench, we can observe it. From London to Tokyo, we've built it.

We have even made a way to examine reality outside of our world. Neil Armstrong and Buzz Aldrin stepped out onto the moon in 1969. [6] They found another hard surface to walk on, but they didn't find paradise.

Could heaven be farther away? April 24, 1990, the Hubble Telescope on board the Shuttle Discovery lifted from earth and into space to begin looking far beyond the moon. [7] We've seen all sorts of pictures beyond our earth. The glimpse has been gratifying. Our experience beyond this planet has been impressive, but we still haven't found how to move to paradise.

Nevertheless, elements of our hard work have paid off. The development of our current civilization has lifted millions from cruelty and poverty to less painful lives. We've come a long way. Billions live longer and easier and safer because of all we've done. However, for all of our energy and improvement, for all of our intelligence and wisdom, for all of our accomplishment, we have never created a Utopian world; we have never built a world without evil.

Can We Buy It?

Maybe a perfect reality is experienced individually. We might attain it by blocking out all the negative things around us and focusing on the positive. By selecting only the finest things in life, we might make our experience with reality the best it can possibly be.

But can we really have pain-free reality through personal skill just by focusing our thoughts on it, by working hard to create it, or, perhaps, by buying it? The problem with all three of these options is that they require us to create a fantasy world around ourselves where we ignore any part of reality that we do not like. Besides, we just discussed building heaven through exploration and hard work, and we've also admitted that these two options have never succeeded in any society. What is true at the social level is also true at the individual level. Whenever we try to manipulate the world around us to create heaven through intelligence and effort, we create as much hell for someone else as we do heaven for ourselves. We become our own incarnation of Hitler, satisfying ourselves and hurting others.

What about buying heaven? That is certainly a third option to consider. You have, no doubt, discovered that paradise isn't available on a store shelf. Department stores don't stock it—try asking the clerks. Online auctions don't offer it. Websites don't sell it. Discount stores don't sell it for less. It doesn't come secondhand in thrift stores.

You can't find heaven listed as a vacation destination in a travel brochure. You can't fly there cheaply on a discount airline. Heaven isn't the eighth continent. Taxes don't pay for it. It isn't a social program or a scientific discovery. It isn't named after some almost-forgotten genius. Heaven is priceless, and that makes it too expensive for a credit card.

All of us are looking for heaven—at least that is what I've found so far. We're looking for heaven in our friends, our food, our houses, our cars, our recreation, our families, and our work. We do our best to "buy" the finest of each one of these that we can, if not with money then with compliments and favors. We're looking everywhere.

We have discovered many good things along the way. We are better off for the search, but we have never succeeded. Each time, we come up short.

Heaven Is Complex

Perhaps our searching, building, and buying doesn't seem to perfect our lives because we are looking for something that is more complex than we expect it to be. You may be satisfied in Yosemite Valley surrounded by mountain scenery until you feel smaller than a lady bug. You may be satisfied in New York's Central Park helping schizophrenics find shelter until you become overwhelmed by the task. You may be satisfied at the board table of a Fortune 500 corporation or peering into an electron microscope until you are left in awe by the marvels of this world.

Intuitively we recognize that we aren't looking for just one "magic pill" to satisfy every person the same way. It isn't about finding just one thing that we will all like. Ultimately, we are seeking to satisfy all of our individual and group needs and wants. We need a "heaven" that is ultimately as complex as all of our human needs and wants combined. We long for *reality* to be *all good*.

For most of us, this intuitive idea of the "the ideal life," "the ideal world," or "a perfect globe" contradicts what we are used to meaning when we use the word "heaven." We are so used to using the word "heaven" dogmatically that we have forgotten it can also refer to those personal and collective desires for a better existence and a better world.

What unites every human being is that internal conception that we want an ideal existence and our drive to obtain individual satisfaction. Whether it's just drinking a glass of water, closing a multi-million dollar real estate deal, taking a snorkeling vacation in Thailand, selflessly giving the shirt off our back, or being recognized and admired at work, every human being is working for the part of "heaven" that appeals to him or her.

Ultimately, our problem with reality as humans is not the complexity of the heaven we intuitively desire but the presence of anything that isn't paradise. Our problem is the existence of injustice, evil, and tragedy. For instance, our problem is those deaths by tigers and malaria while the British mapped southern Asia, not the discovery of the planet's highest mountain. It's the frozen bodies left on the slopes of Mount Everest, not the moment of successful satisfaction when mankind finally arrived at its summit. It's the unkind words and calloused threats we make at the dinner table, not the family members gathered around it. It's the slander and backstabbing at work, not the colleagues we live with each day. It's the broken promises that destroy marriages and businesses, not the people who made those promises in the beginning.

Our problem as humans is that in the midst of all of our complex desires, in the midst of living in a glorious and sometimes dangerous world, we have not discovered anywhere to live without the presence of evil. We have neither built any place that is without evil nor can we focus on what makes us happy and wish evil out of existence. We have to live every day with evil all around us and sometimes in us. We have become so used to this reality that we have given up on the better world we really want. Most of us have given up on the possibility of global bliss because we have experienced too much pain, too much "hell" to believe that heaven is still possible.

By hell, I don't mean an underworld of almost hot fire. Nor am I trying to swear. Anything that diabolically injures us is hell, for hell is what we experience in the presence of evil.

Why Is Evil Still Here?

We haven't gotten rid of the existence of hell on earth because we haven't tamed ourselves. More people around our world suffer from evil that has been introduced and perpetrated by other humans than from all natural disasters combined. Our own species is still the most dangerous creature on the planet. Human character is our last frontier to explore and conquer. We hurt each other. We yell at our kids and our spouses. We ignore our friends. Maybe we steal a little from our boss or our neighbor. We ruin reputations and put others down. We long for some sort of better life and better world, for some sort of heaven, but *we* still create hell.

Most of us aren't cruel all the time. We generally excuse ourselves or think it isn't so bad—at least it isn't for us. However, when we walk a mile in the other people's shoes, putting ourselves in their places, we can in some respect feel life as they experience it. We can learn about their background, what influences them, and how our actions feel to them in order to see ourselves better. When we look at our own actions through the experiences of those around us, our excuses sound very lame.

Honesty requires me to admit that I've been a cause of other people's pain. I am a contributing source of the nastiness that is present in this world. Every man, woman, and child on planet earth has added some kind of anguish to someone at some time.

Probably some of you are talking back to me right now. You start pointing out that there are differences. Showing up late for dinner and disappointing your spouse is not the same as raping an innocent girl. Playing a prank on someone that produces a minor injury isn't the same as using a machete to personally murder hundreds of Rwandan Tutsis for being a little taller and having a distasteful history. Telling your boss you are sick so you can stay home and watch a ball game is nothing like threatening to make an atomic bomb to be used on other countries for letting their women dress in ways you don't approve of.

You are right. There are differences, and those differences are important. Yet those differences don't change the underlying truth that each of these actions contributes to a hellish experience for someone else. We don't have to be the greatest source of torment on earth to be part of its problem. Just because we are not the world's most dangerous monsters doesn't make us great saints.

We have not *found* any location on earth to label, without any qualification, "heaven." We have not *built* anything on earth to label, without any qualification, "heaven." We cannot just focus on the positive or in any other way buy or create an experience that we can label, without any qualification, "heaven." But we can all understand that heaven, whatever that word may mean to us right now, exists wherever hell is absent. Any hellish act, no matter how small, chases away the atmosphere of what we conceive to be heaven.

Right now you and I need an internal change of who we are. We need to eradicate any trace of evil in all of our thoughts and our actions. We need to permanently and completely banish hell. We need something that can solve the heartache in Rwanda after genocide. We need something that can solve the arguments at the dinner table at home. We need something that can remake each one of us so we never again contribute to the needless pain and suffering of another human for the rest of our lives.

We need some kind of heaven that will help us even though we know we cannot discover it, buy it, build it, create it, or imagine it into existence. We need it whether we are strong or weak, rich or poor, kind or cruel. Every human, at least the ones I know, needs and wants heaven. We've been looking for a long time. Naturally, we look for it in the happiest moments of our lives: in food, material belongings, accomplishments, friendships, romance, family, and personal fulfillment.

Most people I know have also given up on finding heaven. We seem to have outgrown that expectation about the time we learned that kissing frogs to turn them into princes is only the suggestion of an overactive imagination.

Before wrestling with a definition of heaven in the next chapter and considering whether or not anything available to us matches that definition, we've spent this chapter examining our search for heaven. What have our disappointments taught us about what is paradise?

The Solution

Our world is wonderful. In the slice of reality that we can live in between the top of Mount Everest and the bottom of the ocean, there is a lot to enjoy and even celebrate. We have much to look forward to discovering, achieving, and experiencing. But as much as we have accomplished, as much as we trust ourselves, as much as we trust our ability to observe and to innovate in order to create a safer environment outside of ourselves (and even here we have a long way to go), we need help to be changed inside ourselves *more* than to transform the world around us. When we look at all of what is real, we recognize that each of us needs something better in life. In other words, we *need* a better reality to be here right now. What we need differs from person to person. No single simplistic solution will solve our problems and satisfy our hearts. To make ourselves and our world a better, happier place requires several changes. These changes go together as a package, and together they form the beginning of heaven. Specifically,

1. We need an attitude and outlook that is realistic, optimistic, and contented; and we need the ability to achieve the greatest success we are capable of reaching.

2. We must find some source of wisdom and strength to change anything that interferes with this attitude and achievement.

3. We must find a way to overcome anything that is hostile to this attitude or interferes with this accomplishment.

4. We must contribute happiness to every relationship we have.

But first let us consider the following questions. Does heaven exist? Will it meet our needs? Is it satisfactory? How does it differ from our current idea of heaven? *What is heaven?*

Chapter 2
THE PROBLEM IS DEFINING HEAVEN

Want a formula for a little trouble? Try five bored boys in a room with nothing to do. Now imagine a hospital ward with twenty-five sick boys stuck in bed with nothing to do. That must be mayhem to the second power.

John made the difference. From the only bed next to the window, he reported the news about life outside of the box. Sunshine cheered the park full of playing children. Rain coaxed out red, purple, yellow, green, and black umbrellas and sent little boys hopping over puddles. Little girls held their mommies' hands on their way to important missions. Dads went to work, and trucks delivered boxes. Happy, healthy people. A world of wonder was outside John's window, and he became the revelator.

Each day twenty-four bored boys waited for the daily news report. Would the little girl who sometimes wore a yellow dress walk her little white dog with a brown ear to the park today? Would the delivery truck leave three, five, or seven boxes at the store across the street? Would the bluebird come early to drink from the pool at the park?

Peter wanted to see the yellow daffodils and the purple iris complement each other so well. He wanted to watch the dog run. So did Benjamin, Scott, Oliver, and twenty other boys, but at least John was at the window. So every day their troubled lives seemed farther away from that one window.

John's reports were strong, but his body was weak. The stronger heaven on earth shone through that window, the tighter hell seemed to grasp his body. Death finally won, and the window bed was empty.

Peter asked for *that* bed. He wanted to bring heaven to the boys as the next *Window Times* reporter. The busy nurses couldn't understand, but Peter was moved anyway.

Peter took his first look through the window into heaven. Would he find the bluebirds easily? Would he recognize the little girl if her dress wasn't yellow and if her dog wasn't with her? Would he count the delivery boxes correctly?

The shock hit Peter like a tornado out of a cloudless sky. He was used to disappointment. He was very sick. He might die. Peter was a brave little boy, but he never expected this. The filthy street. The broken building. The dirt that forgot the beauty of a single flower. No people. Nothing gorgeous. Nothing but an ugly wall across a forgotten street. *What* had John seen?

Slowly Peter realized John's dying gift. That gift was not what John actually saw. What brought John joy was not the dirty street outside or the room full of dying boys inside. John's parting present to the others was how he faced his gloom; how he ignored what was actually outside the window and used his imagination to cheer up the other boys. The dying boy used his last breaths on earth to leave the world around him a better place than he had found it.

For two and a half years, Viktor Frankl lived in the concentration ghettos and camps of World War II era Germany. He was surrounded by the despairing and the dying. He saw humanity at its worst. As a doctor and psychiatrist, he keenly observed the prisoners around him. He watched what made people give up and die and what inspired people to fight and try to live. Not everyone who tried survived. However, all those who gave up, died. He would observe that while we cannot control what happens in our lives, we can control what we feel and what we do about what happens to us. Frankl was able to survive, he wrote, because he had a sense of purpose. [8]

It seems bizarre to look into two different World War II experiences (a hospital ward of dying boys in London and a prisoner's experience in the Auschwitz and Dachau concentration camps more than 500 miles east of London) to find happiness. Perhaps it may not be so odd after all. Both John, the boy revelator, and Viktor Frankl, the educated prisoner, were able to maintain contentment and purpose in painful and frightening places. The terrible circumstances in which they found themselves revealed what was already there. Terrifying situations provide a backdrop that makes the inner human condition stand out in bold relief. These two people in difficult conditions during World War II certainly desired better circumstances, but they did not require any better circumstances in order to be happy or to have a sense of purpose.

We could look at humanity's happiest moments to find heaven. We could go from the hospital room where a newborn baby enters the world, to a world-class concert, to a child's first day of school or recital, to a daughter's wedding day, to the bed where a fetus starts its existence. Still, exciting moments do not guarantee happy people.

Too often humanity demonstrates that they are *not* happy, even under the best of circumstances. We know we have real joy when we can still smile in the worst of circumstances. We know we have real happiness when it can stand up under the harshest scrutiny. It is ironically easiest to discover what makes our lives better when we see humans thriving in the worst circumstances known to mankind.

This is exactly where the greatest hero of the Christian sacred writings stands out. Jesus had the toughest of circumstances, but He made those circumstances the stepping stones to heaven.

Jesus was born in a barn. Herod tried to kill Jesus before He was old enough to think. His older step-brothers constantly gave Him a hard time. Life was tough on Him, but Jesus didn't grow up paranoid. People tried to bully Him, but Jesus never uttered a nasty word. [9]

He was part of the Judean church. That church family was often cruel to Jesus, even trying at various times to trick and hurt Him. For instance, three times in one weekend they tried to murder Him. His own friend, Judas, betrayed Him. Then there was a manipulative trial that had nothing to do with justice, Peter's denial, and a public execution. [10]

Evil set its sights on Jesus and never gave up, and yet, that same evil never made it *inside* of Him. Jesus never said a word or gave a look that was unconscionable. Hell chased Him, surrounded him, ambushed Him, but hell never *conquered* Him. Jesus' life was a constant demonstration that heaven was not *what* happened to Him but *how* He faced what happened to Him. The glory of Jesus was not what happened outside of Him and around Him but what happened inside of Him. Paradise comes first from internal courage and conviction.

Jesus earned the right to tell us about a better reality because He is the ultimate version of ourselves. He operated under more pressure than any of us will ever experience: daily perfection under public scrutiny and in the face of constant opposition. He never drank, never needed an hour on the couch, never paid a psychologist, and never lost his temper. He operated a ministry that didn't need polls and focus groups. Adoration and hatred didn't affect Him. He faced the unthinkable injustice of the death penalty calmly. He lived perfection in our hell, and He taught us to do the same.

If we take a new look at an old story, the ability of Jesus to live contentedly in a discontented world is one of the greatest lessons to humanity. He revealed heaven, not by an abundance of joy, but by dignity in suffering. His life teaches us a new way to live.

This simple Galilean man was in touch with His world, our world. He recognized the challenges and heartaches of each person around

Him. He addressed the ostracization of lepers. He sympathized with the grieving and helped the terminally ill. Still, the dire circumstances did not shake Him. He had a calmer demeanor in Gethsemane, knowing that He was facing a joke of a trial and after that the death penalty, than many of us do if we are an hour late for lunch. Jesus slept in the middle of a raging storm. He went to the temple and sat there, knowing that this very temple was the headquarters of the clergy who were looking for a way to arrest and kill Him. He conducted His work out in the open when it would have been convenient to go into hiding.

We can see in Jesus' example the same strange truth that the dying story teller and Viktor Frankl revealed: we find happiness not in happy circumstances but in personal choices. We find heaven not by looking for it but by demonstrating it. Heaven is a way of life, an act we carry out; it is not the sum total of how the world acts toward us. Heaven is character that is revealed, not the creation of circumstances.

Given Jesus' credibility on the subject, it's worth listening to one of His conversations with the Pharisees. They wanted to know when to look for heaven or, as they were used to saying, "the kingdom of heaven." [11]

Where does Jesus tell us to find heaven? "The kingdom of God cometh not with observation" (Luke 17:20).

You can't see heaven in a travelogue. It won't be covered in a documentary or on the History Channel. Don't expect it to be featured as the next travel destination by any of the major airlines. You can't travel to heaven for a cheaper fare by flying with a discount carrier. It's not a magic destination. Don't look for heaven in palaces or on tropical islands. Don't search for it in faraway places. Heaven isn't hidden in the sand at the beach or on the top of high mountains or at the end of bungees dangling from a bridge. It isn't in a bottle or a can, or served on a plate. It isn't packaged under the name chocolate. Look anywhere you want, you will never find heaven.

"Neither shall they say, Lo here! or, lo there! for, behold, the kingdom of God is within you" (Luke 17:21). Heaven is inside, not outside. It is within, not without. Stop looking. Stop searching. Heaven is not found, it is chosen. Heaven is not what happens to you in life; it is how you face your life. It is the inner life of a human that is lived outwardly, not the outward experiences of life that are reflected inwardly.

The community [12] Jesus advocated is the closest our humanity has ever come to heaven. In His culture, there are no wars and no fights against anyone or anything except evil. There are no hard feelings and no misunderstandings. There is no inferiority and no cruelty. There are no unfair deals and no manipulation. Individual achievement and human relationships are supported and honored. Each human is allowed to grow and thrive to his or her fullest potential. Ambition, discipline, and achievement reach the greatest heights imaginable. In the life and world that Jesus recommends to us, human excellence would be visible everywhere and contentment would be mixed with the satisfaction of accomplishment. This is not the world we live in. Thus, we tend to brush off Jesus' words and go about our lives as though He was just telling stories without any purpose. We consign His statements to a box labeled "Impossible."

We know all too well what our world looks like, and it is a very mixed bag of the good, the bad, and the worst. Human achievement and human foolishness stand hopelessly intertwined. That being the case, we put heaven off into the distant future—far enough away from the present that we do not have to think about it very much.

We decide that heaven is reached only sometime after death. We are sure that heaven has no tsunamis, ice storms, divorce, or danger. We are sure that suicide bombers don't make it there. We are sure that traffic never cuts us off, no one starves, and friends never betray us in heaven. There is no drought and no famine. No computer crashes. No job layoffs. No economic hardships. No foreclosures. THAT is heaven. We are sure it is, and we are sure that we are right.

Jesus knew about a future heaven, and He talked about it as being different than this earth. He taught us to pray that His will be done here on planet Earth the way it is done *in heaven*. Apparently, that heaven and this earth are not the same place. Jesus talked of the angels *in heaven*. Jesus told John of the future heaven where "God shall wipe away all tears from their eyes; and there shall be no more death, neither sorrow, nor crying, neither shall there be any more pain: for the former things are passed away" (Revelation 21:4).

This is a heaven that is not here or now. It is inviting. It is desirable. Nevertheless, it would be spoiled by one person arriving there without the internal choices that make heaven. Pain-free reality does not come by merely changing the weather or the conditions around us. It comes from an absence of any behavior that destroys and injures. It comes from a complete absence of evil, and the presence of evil in our world is something that humans can personally control in themselves.

Jesus tells us of this "other" heaven here right now. "Repent: for the kingdom of heaven is at hand" (Matthew 4:17). Let's put these same words more simply: Repent, heaven is here.

These four words are so profound and different from what we expect, even after 2,000 years of opportunity to reflect on them, that we have trouble hearing what Jesus actually said. Some of us are so used to calling heaven by the title "the kingdom of heaven" that it is difficult to accept the reality that Jesus means "heaven." We are so used to the expression "at hand" that we don't hear Jesus say "here." Others of us are so used to our own belief that heaven is *not* here that we do not accept the declaration of the Expert on heaven that it *is here.*

This powerful expression has been available to us for centuries. There is nothing hidden or secretive about it. But somehow, it has been easy to run right past it as though it never existed. Jesus asked us to complete an action: repent. He justified this action with a reality: heaven is present; it is here. The statement "heaven is here" does not add to His words. It does not take anything away. It simply expresses His words in simple, common language, just as Jesus would have done were He to speak to us in English.

To accept that heaven is present and available right now on planet earth requires that we change our definition of the word. We have to wrap our heads around a new concept of what that word means. We have long believed, more or less, that heaven is a glorious place where good people go sometime in the future. We believed that angels live there and that there are harps and crowns and golden streets and peaceful animals. We believed it is the best real estate in the universe. And there are times that Jesus uses the word to mean all that and more. But there are times that He uses the word very differently.

Jesus told us about things in this heaven that aren't in the hereafter. He told us that heaven is like a field that contained good and bad crops—wheat and a common weed often called a tare. Both grow together in heaven. [13]

The realities of this heaven, which has a good crop spoiled by weeds, are distinct from the realities of the future heaven Jesus described in other passages. The instructions given to the angels to let good and evil temporarily coexist clearly do not refer to the time when there will be no death, neither sorrow, nor crying. The only time and place where good and bad can coexist is right now and right here on earth. Apparently Jesus considered "heaven," as He uses the word, to apply to realities here and now, as well as to very different circumstances in the future.

Jesus used the word "heaven" in the expression "the kingdom of heaven" to refer to more than one thing. He used heaven to refer to character and moral power.[14] He used it to refer to pleasure and convenience and marvelous circumstances, to a specific "geographical" location in the universe.[15]

The ambiguity of using the same term for different experiences has confused people in our world today. We want specificity. In a language with hundreds of thousands of words more than the language Jesus used to speak to mankind 2,000 years ago, and consequently a much greater specificity than was possible two millennia ago, we want the word "heaven" to refer to one specific place or to one specific condition.

Why should we impose on Jesus a clarity that He never meant? He used the term to refer to a complex "formula," a cocktail of place and experience. Why not give Him the benefit of the doubt? After all, He has been to the *location* of heaven, had the *experience* of heaven, and manifested the *character* of heaven. He knows exactly what He is talking about.

If His terminology seems in any way ambiguous today, His life demonstrates a clarity that we would do well to appreciate. If we must put any priority on the different meanings of heaven, Jesus lived the truth that the meaning of character always comes first. He virtually responded to all the attempted "heavens" of paganism and Judaism. To the Greek's wisdom, Jesus challenged that character is more important than wisdom. To the Roman achievement, organization, and ability to negotiate, He challenged that character is more important than achievement, organization, and conflict resolution. To the hedonistic pleasure of other pagans, He asserted that character is more important than pleasure. To the ritualistic and religious behavior of patronizing God lived out by the Hebrew nation, Jesus placed character over claims and ceremonies. To every experiment and counterfeit, Jesus demonstrated that a character of principled love, firm and disciplined mercy, and merciful justice is worth more than any other experience or accomplishment in the universe. Jesus even demonstrated to millions of angels that character is more important than the physical location of heaven and all the joy it contains.

We are not throwing away Jesus' promise to give us good weather, great opportunity, and friends, the best of circumstances and an unlimited life with Him as one of His friends in the future. That check, drawn on The Bank of God's Resources, is one I look forward to cashing when the time comes. But I refuse to throw away the beginning of heaven here and now—the character that Jesus persists in putting first—while I am waiting for a better tomorrow.

Jesus also speaks of the "kingdom of God" and of "eternal life." He used the phrases "kingdom of heaven" and "kingdom of God" interchangeably. He must have meant the same concept by both phrases. Similarly, He used the expression "eternal life" in ways that are perhaps unfamiliar to us but are identical with the expressions "kingdom of God" and "kingdom of heaven." [16]

The biblical use of the expressions heaven, kingdom of heaven, kingdom of God, and even eternal life are very different than the meanings we give to them today. I have chosen to abandon our modern conceptions of these words in this book and ask what happens if we look at our daily existence in light of those old, divinely offered meanings of these same words. Rather than use each of these expressions, I have adopted the one most common in our modern language, "heaven." I have adopted the somewhat ambiguous meaning for the word "heaven" that includes character, power, experience, location, and future glory all in one. [17]

We can confidently accept this use of the word heaven when we see that Paul also understood the terms used by Jesus for heaven to refer to an experience we should have right now. "The kingdom of God [i.e., heaven] is not food and drink but righteousness and peace and joy in the Holy Spirit" (Romans 14:17 RSV). The apostle was not talking about a location. Paul clearly understood the term "kingdom of God" to refer to an experience here on earth made possible by a divinely supplied power and wisdom.

This heaven found here on earth is not circumstantial. It does not come with money or by birth. You can't get it by words or actions. You can't earn it. You can't bribe God into giving it to you. Heaven isn't given away randomly to good boys and good girls. There is no form of manipulation or of denigrating demand that works with God. Heaven comes only to those who ask God with humility. [18] "Ask, and it will be given it to you" (Matthew 7:7). That is simply the only way to get it, and it is the asking part where we have trouble.

Asking is difficult for us because it requires us to let go of part of ourselves in order to get heaven. We have to let go of our evil desires, our pride, our self-flattery, our ego, our vanity, and our insistence that we are right. We have to accept that God is right and let ourselves depend on Him completely. To receive heaven, we have to give up hell. Jesus called this experience of letting go of hell repentance [19], that is, a dissatisfaction with our own hellish behavior, a sorrow for our self-de-structive habits and thoughts, and a humility and conciliation toward all those whom we have injured unfairly. Heaven is the power to do these things and more. Heaven is the power to face and change our attitudes, our habits, and ultimately our circumstances.

A few of those ancient Bible stories illustrate this heaven. Joseph grew up as his father's pet and his brothers' pest. When they saw a chance, his older ten brothers sold him as a slave to be taken to Egypt. The brothers solved their own problem by getting rid of Joseph, but they created a problem for their father. Jacob mourned deeply for his son who, he was told, was dead.

Approximately twenty years later, the group of brothers traveled to Egypt to buy food. Without their realizing it, the highest official of Egypt understood their language and recognized them as his estranged brothers. Joseph used his disguise to hold his brothers accountable, but he never took the opportunity to get even with them. After testing them to determine how safe it was to reveal himself, he finally opened up. Then, after personally revealing his true identity, he sent them back to move his father and all their families to be his guests in the best part of Egypt. He treated them with honor and privilege after they had treated him with disgust and hatred.

Heaven was not exhibited in how Joseph was treated by his family when they sold him to migrant slave traders. Heaven was revealed in how Joseph treated his family. Hated, sold, forsaken, he didn't get full revenge when he saw them again. Heaven for Joseph was the power[20] to be hard on his brothers without ever taking revenge or taking advantage of them. Heaven gave him the power to give his brothers the best place in Egypt and to help with the moving costs after they had sold him as a slave. Joseph was gracious when abused, cheerful when enslaved, and honest under pressure. Paradise was not how his brothers Rueben, Judah, Simeon, Levi, Gad, Issachar, or any of the others treated Joseph. Heaven provided Joseph with the power to live heavenly when his brothers treated him like hell.

The Persian prime minster, Daniel, was betrayed by his employees, who used his own name and reputation against him.[21] The presidents and princes argued in his name for a national law outlawing his religious practices. Daniel was threatened with the death penalty for the same habit of praying that he had practiced for decades. Still, he prayed openly. As a result, Daniel was thrown to lions for dinner. Heaven was what gave Daniel the ability to be in the lion's den without a curse in his heart or his mouth. Miraculously, the lions skipped dinner, so they were even hungrier for breakfast the next morning; breakfast made from Daniel's troublesome employees. Daniel was so filled with heaven that it mattered not how work treated Daniel; heaven pervaded how Daniel worked.

Job's riches and his friends were not the essence of heaven for him. Neither could heaven be experienced working on the farm and in the shipping business, nor in being a grandpa, as satisfying as all of these were. Heaven was revealed in how Job handled losing his family, his wealth, and his friends at the same time. Heaven was uncovered when there was sorrow without hatred, acceptance of difficulties without bitterness.

Returning to Persian history, heaven was not to be found in Esther being elevated to queen of the richest and most powerful nation on earth at that time. It wasn't seen in the summer palace, the winter palace, or in all the servants. It was observed in Esther's courage in telling her husband who her family really was at a time when they were the most unpopular group in the kingdom. It was witnessed in her bravery in standing up for the helpless when doing so could have cost her not only her throne but also her life. Heaven was manifested in her willingness to reveal her Jewish heritage for the first time only after the Jews were condemned nationally to be exterminated; in her choice to stop genocide by exposing herself as one of its actual targets.

Heaven was demonstrated in the courage exhibited by thousands of martyrs over the centuries when they faced the end of life. Seeing there was no escape, they purposefully walked to their own death. Some of them went singing. Being burned to death, torn into pieces, or whatever other cruelty they faced was not enough to steal contentment from their hearts or joy from their lips.

The heroes of the Bible and of history show that heaven was revealed in how they faced life, not in how life treated them. Heaven was not seen in how wealthy or healthy they were, how their families and friends behaved toward them, how their marriages worked, or how death ignored them. People who demonstrated heaven in these situations displayed an inner calm, self-control, dignity, and nobility. They were heroes for living bigger than their circumstances. In the winter moments of life, they seemed to live in a perpetual summer. Treated unjustly, they were still just. Attacked unfairly, they were fair in return. They lived an attitude, a character, a perspective, a life that was a manifestation of heaven.

Heaven today is exhibited in how you love your spouse, not in how your spouse loves you. Heaven can be seen in how you love your children and grandchildren, not in how they love you. Heaven is evidenced in how you face family that loves or family that hates you. Heaven is manifested in how you live whether friends support or betray you. Heaven is demonstrated in what you give to work as well as what you do to work well and hard at your employment, not in what your employer pays you. Heaven is illustrated in how you face poverty or wealth without being a slave to either. To paraphrase famous words, heaven is what you give to your country, not what your country gives to you. *Heaven is how you face life, not what you get from it.*

In a time when our world is focused on rights and equality for *me*, heaven can raise us above the injustices we experience, making us more content and constant than our circumstances ever justify. It instills in us an internal attitude, fortitude, and character rather than leading us to focus only on how we are treated and on those who haven't been fair to us. Heaven imparts to us the internal discipline to "do no harm," the personal attitude to always be content, and the personal commitment to act for the benefit of all who are potentially affected by our influence.

Here is where many of us stop. We realize that heaven is *not* who we have been. Righteous and courageous people like Esther, Job, and Joseph certainly reflected a better way of life than we are used to living. Daniel and Noah exuded heaven from their lives. Jesus was heaven in human form. Yet we tell ourselves that heaven is not in us. *I wasn't born like them. Don't these Bible heroes resonate with the heavenly because they are different from me? They were good people. Their problems weren't like my problems. They weren't like me. I can't be good like them. I can't mirror all things heavenly. I was born with the wrong genes, the wrong DNA.*

We use every argument we can find. I used to comfort myself with these common excuses. It was the easiest way to make myself feel good when I knew I was failing. It was an attitude of spiritual defeat.

We're all very much like this in that this is the way we talk to ourselves when we abandon our manhood or womanhood in yielding to a perception of being morally helpless. But before we give up as a group of moral losers, let us see whether or not we are really so helpless. Is our defeatism justified by anything but our own spiritual laziness?

If you are telling me that internal discipline and contentment are impossible in a world of chaos, then you must have at least tried. If you are telling me that behaving nobly toward others is impossible when you are treated unfairly, then you must be speaking from the experience of failure—for most of us have truly attempted. We wanted to be better than our circumstances. We wanted to do and to be well.

Unfortunately, it didn't work, and it is this trying and failing that discourages us. We grow confused only to look around us and see that others look like they have already given up. So we reshape our beliefs about the world around us. We decide that whatever we haven't accomplished can't be accomplished.

This is an old human song. People told the Wright brothers that no one could fly because they were speaking from experience. So why try? But Orville and Wilbur didn't give up.

Humans at one point believed they couldn't build a bridge across the San Francisco Bay. They had in their minds that they couldn't build tall skyscrapers or go to the moon. Over and over, we placated ourselves with the assurance that what hasn't been done can't be done at all. No one could do it; then it was done by people who refused to settle for too little. This should teach us that our own attitudes and beliefs hold us back.

My father used to tell me, "If you say you can't, you are right." We fulfill our own prophecy. Most of us find living in the hope of heaven to be impossible because we believe it is impossible. We must be careful about believing in our own impossibilities, for that belief might well be the very source of evil, the origin of our falling into the pit of hell. It might be how we create our own moral self-destruction.

The idea that we humans cannot do what is moral and noble all the time projects a terrible image of God. If He gives out heaven to some people who are naturally "good" and then refuses to help anyone who finds morality and nobility and integrity difficult, we assume He is just playing favorites. If God only cares about and helps the best of us, then He is not a God of love and compassion but one of injustice and unfairness.

Let us be very careful not to accuse God of being partial. In the process, we may set ourselves up to fail and at the same time accuse God of being evil. When we say that heaven is only for special people, we are really arguing that God has pets. He will give heaven only to his pets, and the rest of us will just miss out. If that is really what God is like, it is little wonder that most of us don't love Him very much.

Just because this view is popular is no reason to believe that God is filled with favoritism. We pride ourselves on rejecting myths and living by evidence. Yet we cling endlessly to myths of God as an unjust Being who hands out the good things in life to provide a heaven on earth to His favorites. We then use these myths as an excuse to give up on achieving heaven before we even really try to find it.

Jesus, our proven authority on all things heavenly, taught that heaven is for everyone. Jesus, the member of the Godhead who once was visible, told us that His Father, an invisible member of the Godhead, sent Him that everyone might have eternal life, which (as previously mentioned) is just another way of saying heaven. John 3:16 is the most famous and quoted passage in the entire Bible. Let's stop mumbling it as if it were some intellectually empty mantra and actually take it at face value. Jesus offers that gift to you and me today. *He* says it's for everyone. Let's stop arguing with *Him*. There is not a passage in the Bible that says heaven isn't for you as long as you are willing to let go of your own pride, selfishness, bitterness, manipulative tendencies, and nastiness, submitting it all to God. Heaven is available to everyone willing to accept it. That is all that's required.

How we face life is how we accept heaven. Heaven gives us the power to change our habits. Heaven is our source of contentment and certainty in any circumstance. Heaven opens to us the ability to recognize that we are blessed even when it seems like we may be cursed. Heaven is choosing the best attitude in every moment, making the best of every situation.

And the problem we all face is that this heaven isn't here for most of us. So how do we find it?

Chapter 3
GETTING HEAVEN

O thniel played in the sand with his cars. He had a whole town near his father's garden. The grocery store was close to the carrots. The barbershop was close to daddy's row of peas. The mechanic was next to the potatoes. Home was at the end of the tomatoes.

While daddy weeded his garden, Othniel played in his town. He drove a red car from the barber to the mechanic. Then he drove to the grocery store to buy lunch, but he couldn't drive from the grocery store to home because there was a rock in his way.

"No problem," Othniel thought to himself, "I will move the rock. He pulled, but it did not move; He pushed but it did not budge. He pulled harder; then he pushed harder. Still, the rock was stubborn. Othniel got mad. Tears showed up in his little blue eyes and then succumbed to gravity. He sat down on the troublesome rock. What could he do?

Daddy had been watching from the garden. He saw the road building and the roadblock. He walked over to Othniel and knelt down next to his son. Tenderly, he asked, "What happened?"

Othniel poured his heart out, knowing his dad could fix things.

"I was driving back from the grocery store with lunch. The people at home are hungry. I need to get there with the food. Daddy, they all are going to starve to death. I can't get home. I *can't* drive there. This rock is IN MY WAY!"

Dad had to hide his smile at Othniel's imagination. He also knew that he had an opportunity to teach Othniel a lesson. So he asked, "Why didn't you move the rock?"

Puzzled, Othniel sobbed, "I tried, but I *caaaaan't!*"

"I know you can."

"I can't."

"You tried?"

"Yes. I tried, Daddy. It's too big."

"Did you try your best?"

Othniel's eyes grew large. "Daddy, I *tried* my *very* **best**."

"I don't think so."

Then Othniel became angry.

"I did. I pushed that old rock as hard as I know how, but it won't go anywhere. I really can't push this rock. It's too hard. I **can't** move *this rock!*"

"Son, you did not try your hardest."

Othniel was shocked at his father's words. What did he mean? How could *he* try harder? What more could he do? His blues eyes looked up at his father as if to ask, *What do you mean?*

Dad reached down and gave Othniel a hug. "Son, you've never tried your hardest until you ask me for help."

Just because I've grown up doesn't mean that I've grown too old for the advice given to Othniel. When my dearest friend betrayed me, costing me thousands of dollars and much heartache, I was angry. Tears streamed down my face. I couldn't sleep at night. I hurt. It was so unfair. My suffering wasn't because of some imaginary rock in the dirt. My family and friends were losing money and relationships over my friend's lies. I wanted someone to make it right. I wanted justice. I wanted to feel whole again. I wanted it all to go away. Yet all my wanting did nothing for me. Bitterness, anger, and sorrow did anything but make me happy. Nothing could be done. My friend was too selfish to make it right.

I could go on with life, just not with the life I had previously planned to live. I understood that the sooner I accepted my new situation, the better it would be for me.

However, I just couldn't take that step and accept what happened. My friend's injustice was like a rock. I couldn't move it. Nothing I did would get rid of it. I worked all day and climbed into bed at night. When my mind was no longer distracted by responsibility, it was consumed with grief and anger. The more I tried to push that anger out of my life, the more it looked like it was there to stay forever. It seemed like there was no other possibility left. I needed help. I tried as hard as I could to push and pull that grief and anger out of my life, but it would not budge. Then I did my best: I turned to my Father, and He helped me.

This wasn't the first time I had asked for His help. When I was a teenager, I couldn't pull my dreamy head out of my imagination and get to work. As an adult looking back on my childhood, I realize that my younger self wanted to feel the affection my paranoid schizophrenic mother never gave me. I wanted the attention I felt I was missing So the easiest way to get out of that hole in my life, that sorrow in my heart, was to daydream of something more comfortable. I suppose my "drug" of choice was relatively harmless as it did little to deteriorate my body. It never made me lose my mind, but it also meant I was good for nothing when it came to work. I couldn't get a job or schoolwork done when I felt like daydreaming.

I tried every mental trick to stop daydreaming that my young mind could invent. They were all a waste of time. I still couldn't control myself. So this became the first time I ever asked the God I had been taught about as a child for help. I certainly didn't know how to ask Him. I wasn't used to talking to an Invisible Being. In school they don't teach you how to do that. I've never discovered "How to Talk to God 101" in a syllabus. I didn't have any experience in how to control my day-dreaming. I just needed help. I needed to be able to control *all* of myself. I needed to change my habits and feelings. I needed the strength to move on from loss and pain, forgive, and put things into perspective. I needed help from someone wiser than I had ever met. I cried out into the darkness even though I didn't know if God would pay any attention to me. I was desperate and willing to try whatever it took.

Both times, I received my answer from the Invisible. I found the strength and ability to forgive. I found the wisdom to put my pain in perspective. I found a way to become stronger despite my loss. I found a way to process both injustice and pain every time either one came knocking on my door. I found a source of consistent contentment. I got this kind of help only from the Divine.

Dialogue with the Invisible

I never set out to become friends with an Invisible Person. This Divine Ghost found me and introduced Himself to me. That simple introduction in the middle of the night, years ago, was unique. He changed my perception of life, my standard of achievement, and my optimism. He became the source of the happiest moments I've ever experienced.

I have a very skeptical mind, so I don't believe things very easily. When others think they have found the truth, I am still asking questions and testing hypotheses. I was born skeptical, and I only get worse as time goes by. So you can imagine that I was doubtful when my unseen Friend tried to get in touch with me. He kept trying to get my attention in an invisible way, and I kept ignoring Him. I can understand if you are suspicious also.

In fact, I recognize that it is not easy to explain how to be best friends with an Invisible Being in our age of pragmatism. No one thinks ghosts and spirits can meet the test of scientific observation. You can't put a ghost in a test tube and do lab experiments. So people think it's a little psychologically strange to have an Invisible Being for a friend. We don't put visible beings in a test tube just to be sure that they exist. So why would we make such a demand on an invisible one?

People wonder, "Aren't you just talking with yourself? Isn't that Divine Ghost just your own imagination?"

Well, I wish my imagination were that smart. I wish I could talk to myself and get the same contentment, guidance, and companionship. It never works that way, however. I've tried. I'm simply not bright enough to come up with the ideas and solutions I have gotten from this Invisible Being.

The Divine Invisible Being is the only one who has always offered me comfort. He has always offered explanations of what life is about. He has been my source of understanding when I couldn't figure out the problems of life. He has been my encouragement and my mentor. He is the only One who has ever given me the consistent ability to control my emotions, change my habits, and change my attitude. He has constantly given me the wisdom to always find a way that is good for everyone.

I have decided that I don't want to live without His companionship and nurture. Nothing else has ever offered the satisfaction He has. No one else has provided me the solutions to my problems in life the way He has.

I found Him in the hardest moments of my history, and He never left me to thrash about during those events. He continually nurtures and instructs me to the point where I've come to live in a continual state of gratitude.

Words are some of the most enjoyable "objects" in my life, yet I cannot find the adequate words to explain the feeling of perpetual contentment and joy. This has to be felt to be understood. I've never found a single human experience comparable to the excitement from discovering the hints of the Invisible Being at work. Even then, I have the sneaking suspicion that I am only touching the tip of the proverbial iceberg while the greatness and richness of being blessed still lies hidden from my sight, just waiting to be discovered.

I've come to believe that, like Othniel in the story, no one has ever done his or her personal best until he or she has asked God for help. We may be successful, very successful by the standards of our contemporary world. We may be popular, but I think that we could be even greater if only the "rocks" were out of our way.

For some of us, the rocks in our lives are circumstances that hold us back from achievement. For others, it is the lack of nurture and mentorship. Still others live in the blessings of opportunity and support. Regardless, all of us still do things we regret. It may be a little lie told to a spouse or girlfriend to hide the pictures on our computer or impatience with our child. It may be the tone of our voice at work. It may be something far worse. No matter the issue, each of us has those internal contradictory wishes.

No one else has ever resolved for me this great internal contradiction we all face. That contradiction became clear to me while reading the Bible. Jesus spoke of heaven as being internal and organically part of who we are. [22] He never identified heaven by ethnicity, talent, success, or membership. He compared it to trees. An apple tree always bears apples. Those apples may be red or yellow or green. They may taste sweet or sour, but they are apples. We don't find pineapples, potatoes, or Brussels sprouts growing on an apple tree. We just find apples. It doesn't matter what label you use for the fruit, the tree still produces apples. Jesus taught us clearly that when we have heaven within us, we act like heaven. When we don't have heaven, nothing else can replace it. You can't fake it or get around it.

That is just the problem Jesus observed. You either have heaven or you don't. I wasn't born with heaven in my soul. Injustice devastates me. I have no secret supply of sweetness. I get frustrated just like anyone else. I've said things that hurt other people.

I still want heaven, however. I want to be an "apple tree," and all I seem to grow sometimes are "onions." What I want to do doesn't happen; what I do not want to do happens.

I am not alone. We do not get married just to have an opportunity to go through divorce. We want companionship to last. We get married in the hope of lasting happiness, but over and over again, the joy doesn't last. Marital bliss dissipates so often that some become cynical and give up on ever being happy.

We don't bring children into the world hoping they will insult us. We do not make business agreements with the hope that the other person will break the agreement. We don't plant apple trees and expect to harvest only onions.

So there we see the contradiction. We want a perfect world, but we don't act perfectly. You cannot have a perfect world if you do not act perfectly. We ruin our own pretty pictures. This contradiction is another of the "rocks" we need to have removed. Our actions should always contribute to a perfect world. The fact that they don't is clear proof that we need the help of Someone big enough to move our rocks.

As soon as I mention perfection, I am afraid that I will scare some of my readers. Many have lived in an imperfect world and given up all hope of perfection. It has become almost a religious doctrine in our age to believe perfection is a dangerous and impossible idea.

It is true that many of the most perilous moments of world history have been created by individuals on a mission to perfect *others* or else get rid of them. Jesus warned us of those who believe they are doing God a favor by killing people who disagree with them. [23] It is true that many have injured themselves by trying to force "perfection." If the forcing of "perfection" has caused so much harm in human history, is there any room for true perfection left?

We don't need theology or philosophy to find the answer. We only need to look around. Humanity is relentlessly trying to live in a "perfect" world. Each of us works hard to create a perfect world as close as possible around ourselves. For so many of us, it is one of our most passionate and persistent pursuits. If perfection is overrated and dangerous, why do we so constantly strive for it? None of us are willing to contentedly accept our imperfect world. If we were happy with life as it is, we would never have a need to change it. We wouldn't need competition. We could all relax and coast. Implicit in every attempt to improve or change our world is an acceptance of and desire for perfection as an ultimate goal. And that desire for perfection is really a desire for heaven.

We can *never force* heaven on ourselves or on any other person; neither does heaven force itself on us. We will never have this heaven of perfection as long as our own actions continue to contribute to an imperfect world.

There is the internal contradiction of life—we each want a world that is better than the one that exists around us as the result of our own actions. This is the contradiction that Jesus has solved for me. I can change my own beliefs, attitudes, and actions by consulting the Divine Invisible Being. I can find ways to contribute to a better life, ways that satisfy every part of me, down to my deepest core. Slowly, I can change who I am. I can stop making the world around me worse than the one I want to live in.

How do we start getting heaven? If we don't have heaven, where do we get it? Since none of us started out by having heaven around us, how do we change mid-stream? How do we change from "onions" into "apples"? What does it take to get heaven?

How to Get Heaven

Heaven is a gift we can only get from God and by His help. We can improve our lives through human effort, through education, by becoming more cultured, and through the exercise of our will power. All of these have an important place in our world and in our lives, but they cannot change who we are. They cannot remake us from onions into apples. In this transformation, these attributes are completely powerless. Effort, education, culture, and willpower may produce a performance of publicly correct behavior, but they cannot change our thoughts, our ideas, our attitudes, and our hearts. They cannot purify the springs of life. There must be a power working from within, a new life from God, before men can be changed from evil to decent and noble perfection. The only power that can make this change is Christ. His grace alone can quicken the lifeless faculties of the soul and attract it to God, to holiness.

Every human acts cruelly at some point, at some time. It may not happen very often, but it happens. Everyone reaches the point where hell comes out in our words, our attitudes, and our actions. We feel that we can't help it, so we need power to change our habits. Education, will power, time, and money aren't enough. We need extra-human power. We need divine power.

Thank God that His heaven is here now. The *power* of heaven is here. The *wisdom* of heaven is here. The *strength* of heaven is here. The *contentment* of heaven is here. You can have it now. It is free *just for the asking*. You don't have to pay for it. In fact, you can't pay for it. You don't have to beg and whine for it. You don't have to have talent for it. All you have to do is ask and keep asking. Never stop asking until you get all the moral power and wisdom you need. You and I can move every rock in our lives if we only ask the Divine Invisible Being to help us.

Maybe you are so used to the word "heaven" referring to a place that you never thought about it as a power inside of us to change us. Jesus told us about heaven as a personal power. "Heaven is like unto leaven, which a woman took, and hid in three measures of meal, till the whole was leavened" (Matthew 13:33).

Jesus uses the analogy of yeast to describe heaven. Yeast makes up a small percentage of the ingredients in bread, dwarfed by all the flour and water. Though there is only a tiny amount of yeast in making bread, it is at the same time the strongest ingredient. Yeast is the power that changes flour into bread and does not leave the bread dough as just a brick. Yeast's activity also takes time.

Heaven is like yeast in our lives. Our commitment of time to listen to God and think about Him has a powerful influence in making us "palatable." Accepting Him will change us. An "hour" of prayer a day (that includes studying the Bible and talking to God while we study our own lives and life itself) will, little by little, over time, make a huge change for the better in any personality by connecting the soul to the God of heaven.

> "As many as received Him, to them gave He power to become the sons of God, even to them that believe on His name: which were born, not of blood, nor of the will of the flesh, nor of the will of man, but of God" (John 1:12, 13).

Jesus had the power of heaven in His heart—the power to make moral choices, the power to control His emotions, the wisdom to find the best course of action, and the power to carry it out. Jesus never let injustice take the power of heaven out of Him.

An unfair trial, lying witnesses, and an unjust death sentence couldn't take away the peace that heaven offers. Neither the hatred of friends and enemies nor the sins of the world could steal that peace from His heart. Through it all, Jesus behaved in a heavenly fashion. His character demonstrates that heaven is possible and thereby makes all of our hellish behavior merely an excuse. Hanging on the infamous cross, Jesus never let hell banish heaven from His thoughts and feelings. Jesus lived through hell and still behaved like heaven.

How can we put Him through hell all over again? How can we disappoint Him and disrespect Him like that? We receive the offer of heaven from Him, yet we give Him hell in return. Why do we do that? Our behavior is such an injustice!

Jesus offers us the power to change any wrong habit we have ever had. Jesus offers us the power to change any wrong attitude any time we ask Him. Jesus offers us the wisdom to understand and solve any problem we may ever have.

"I am not ashamed of the gospel of Christ: for it is the power of God unto salvation to every one that believeth" (Romans 1:16). Jesus offers us heaven just for asking.

And yet, there is more to asking. Heaven "is like a jewel merchant who is in quest of choice pearls. He finds one most costly pearl; he goes away; and though it costs all he has, he buys it" (Matthew 13:45, 46 *Weymouth New Testament*). Asking Jesus to give us heaven goes with a willingness to give up the things that hold us back. If our attitudes keep us locked in hell, we must to let go. If our wrong habits keep us in the prison of hell, we have to let go. Jesus only gives us heaven when we give up hell. We can never have both. It's one or the other. We have to choose which one we want. Anytime we are willing to give up our hell, Jesus will put heaven inside of us. But we have to let go first. Surrender is about completely letting go. If we don't let go, we won't have any room inside for heaven to exist in our hearts.

Heaven Is Being Mentored by God

Heaven is more than power and wisdom from God. It's also His mentorship. It is actually hearing His ideas. Heaven is the assurance that comes from knowing we can always listen to Him and His wisdom. It is feeling secure in knowing He is always available for help and advice. It is basking in the sense of strength and joy fueled by this assurance and security. It is thrilling to one of the strongest human emotional experiences possible, an experience that sweeps away *every* human insecurity.

Maybe you are going to tell me that listening for God is a strange idea. Most of us believe in God. Most of us will admit to talking to God at some point. We've become quite good at talking *at* Him when we feel helpless and that we really need Him. Some of us even talk *to* Him all the time. We can become rather absorbed in our monologue. Nobody, however, claims to hear God, except maybe some of those in the mental hospital, and no one believes they heard God. We call their conversations delusions. So if anyone claims to hear God, we start explaining it away. We resort to skepticism. In our day, most of us doubt anyone who claims to have heard God.

(A few of us go the other way. When we *want* to believe that we have actually heard God, we resort to trickery: we claim we have heard God with every impression or feeling we get. We project ourselves onto God, which leads us to attribute to Him ideas and actions that are bizarre and sometimes a little embarrassing. So most of us avoid the awkwardness and embarrassment and don't even discuss the topic.)

Then we find a little problem when we look at the Bible. That book is full of stories of people who heard God. Abraham moved to another country because he heard God. The whole Jewish nation moved because Moses heard God. Cain argued with God after he committed murder. Even the non-religious Pharaohs of Egypt and the kings of Babylon got messages from God. The Bible says that God talks. It doesn't say that He talks only to good or holy people. It says that He talks!

We could disregard the Bible. We might call it outdated and ignore it as many do. Yet doing so causes another problem. The Bible makes some statements that are simply hard to ignore. While it's true that a few Bible stories seem a little gruesome when you first read them, other ideas in the Bible are too good to throw away. The idea that heaven is inside of us, not on television, is too good an idea to trash. The idea that the measure of men or women is how they treat others rather than how they are treated is too good an idea to disregard. [24] The idea that humility is preferable to humiliation is too good an idea to dump. [25] The idea that we should value those who hurt us rather than hate them is too good an idea to abandon. [26] The Bible simply has material that we need and cannot afford to throw away. It stands as the oldest and most influential book in the world to teach us to tolerate those who are different than us.

The Bible contains things that are unusual and even priceless. Will we reject the ideas of the Bible because it describes some things we have never seen or that seem strange to us? Will we destroy the rose because it grows on a bush with thorns?

Certainly, no more faith is required to accept the concepts given to us by the Bible, even though we cannot understand or explain all of its contents, than is required to trust science, the opinions of experts, or any other book considered holy. We can't understand or explain everything science tells us, but we trust it anyway. Experts contradict each other. Who is wise enough to know what truth is when the experts cannot agree? Yet we trust them anyway. Other books that are considered holy require us to trust ideas that we do not understand or have the ability to explain. Why are we so willing to depend on science, on experts, and even on other religions to understand questions about the reality of life? Why do we hold the Bible to a different standard than we use for any other source of truth?

Every source that we trust to tell us what is reality and truth has things we cannot understand or explain. Yet some people reject the Bible for just that reason. Ignoring the Bible because we find its contents challenging is prejudice, not open-mindedness. I've chosen to take a second look at the idea of hearing God. Consider what we can discover when we open ourselves up to the possibility that God will communicate with us.

Hearing in the Silence

An analogy will explain how I've learned to identify the voice of God. I mentioned that my mother was different from other mothers. She never hugged me, comforted me, or cried—at least in my memory—until she lay dying. Helpless on her bed, she couldn't talk above a mumble. She could not walk. I didn't know whether she recognized me or not until I touched her shoulder and tears came to her eyes.

Those tears changed me. Deep inside of me, I always longed for my mother's emotions. I couldn't always explain what I longed for, but I wanted her to hold me, to love me, to cuddle me. I wanted her to tell me that I was important and that everything would be alright. I wanted something that never happened. She told me how bad I was; she didn't touch me, smile at me, or show any emotions except anger—until those tears. [27] Her tears spoke what her voice never could and never will. My mother's tears that afternoon were the most important communication I ever received from her. She said what I needed to hear most *without moving her lips or making a sound.*

Her tears aren't the only silent message I've received. The look on my father's face often told me what words could never communicate. His sympathy, his joy, his sorrow, his curiosity, his love—all those shouted from his face. His words often only whispered those things to me as his way was to speak in an understated manner. His voice gave me ideas, encouragement, and advice. His face showed me his heart. Much of the person I am in this world, I owe to my father's face.

It's not only my mother's tears and my father's face that talked to me. My father's character did also. Years after his death, his character still speaks to me. I still live for his smile. I still recognize his advice, although he cannot say anything. I knew him so well that even now I know what he would tell me in any situation. I still hear my father telling me simple truths like, "Two wrong actions don't make a right one." His life still speaks to me long after his voice is dead.

Others also influence me today. I sometimes think of Abraham Lincoln and remember learning about his wisdom when he told stories. George Washington inspires me to be humble at all times. Martin Luther King, Jr. teaches me that we must look at our present moment, admit our faults, and challenge those faults in light of the Scriptures. Thousands of martyrs who died for believing differently from the majority have left their legacy of courage so that I might stand firm in my own beliefs even when others won't. That legacy whispers to me to treat with respect those who disagree with me, regardless of the outcome.

We are surrounded by the voices of people who have long been silent. Sometimes we lose the sound of these silent voices in the bustle of life. Our current noise drowns out their messages. Thus, there are deep truths that are only found in the still moments in life when we hear the silent speech of others.

Sometimes in the silence I even think I recognize the voice of a "silent" God. His voice has never thundered at me from the heavens. At no time has His sound called to me from a cloud. I don't know what it's like to shake His hand. I've never seen His hair color. I've never looked into His eyes. I've never smelled His skin. I've never heard the sound of God's voice. Nevertheless, like my mother's tears and my father's facial expressions, I've understood His message without hearing Him speak.

The Voice of God

Knowing whether or not I have heard God accurately can be a difficult question. How do we recognize the voice of God? Our first problem when we try to hear Him is that we can't see God. Our second problem is that we don't generally hear an audible voice. How do we solve these two problems?

Incidentally, Jesus said in John 16:7, "It is better I leave you so that the Divine Invisible Being can talk to you." [28] Jesus' statement provides us with the same challenge. How do we hold a conversation with an Invisible Being? How does He talk to us? How can we experience this promise of Jesus?

The Divine Invisible Being "talks" through other people, through various circumstances, and through impressions. Let me give you an example by telling you how Christianity first addressed intolerance.

Christianity began as a church of individuals with love, nurture, and support for each other, but it imported certain faults that threatened to ruin the church. Jews of that time were famous for treating non-Jews as second-class citizens. Jewish Christians inherited a certain amount of intolerance from the Jews, so they too treated non-Jewish Christians as second-class people. "There arose a murmuring of the Grecians against the Hebrews, because their widows were neglected in the daily administration" (Acts 6:1). Even worse, some of the Jewish Christians only wanted other Jewish Christians to be church members. "Certain men which came down from Judea taught the brethren, and said, Except ye be circumcised after the manner of Moses, ye cannot be saved" (Acts 15:1).

The message against intolerance came directly from Jesus at first He visited the rejected people: Samaritans, Gentiles, tax collectors prostitutes, and criminals. Jesus made friends with whomever wasn't part of the "brown-eyed" Jews. He lived a life of non-discrimination. As I mentioned, when He went back home to heaven, He left the Divine Invisible Being as the agent of communication with the invisible Godhead: "I have yet many things to say unto you, but ye cannot bear them now. Howbeit when he, the Spirit of truth, is come, he will guide you into all truth" (John 16:12, 13).

It took a little while for those early Christians to adjust from one Teacher to Another. They had to learn to recognize the message of the Spirit of truth.

The message of the Divine Invisible Being can be noticed because *He repeats Himself until we get the point.* In fact, often it is the *repetition* that finally gets through to us. (Have you ever realized that something is a good idea and then later also realized that you had made the same conclusion at an earlier time? Maybe Someone was trying to get through to you.)

The Divine Invisible Being started with Simon Peter. Good old talkative Peter. The Divine Invisible Being gave Peter a dream so strange that Peter couldn't make any sense of it. In fact, God gave the disciple that strange dream as a message to warn Peter not to discriminate against his own guests who were just about to arrive.

Peter heeded this warning. Otherwise it probably would have just scared him to open the door and find people there whom he had never met, yet who knew about him. Instead, Peter accepted the message given to him in his dream and went home with his guests.

This visit was life-changing for Peter. His new friends demonstrated that they were ready to be church members. He found that his prejudice against these non-Jews could not stand in the face of the dream he witnessed. Against all of his past habits of discrimination, Peter welcomed them into the church.

Peter overcame his ethnic prejudice, but his old church friends were shocked and offended. So Peter had to tell his bizarre story to his colleagues and supporters over and over again. Some got it, others didn't. Some got it without Peter's story. Some never got it at all. Thus, a big controversy was created in the Christian church, threatening to split the church in half—the tolerant versus the intolerant. The love of Jesus was disappearing in this internal war.

To find common ground, reach unity, and calm the controversy, a convention was called to take place in Jerusalem. In that convention, Peter told the story of his dream and his experience—an angel, a dream, a family that belonged in the church—to justify giving up intolerance toward non-Jews. How could Peter argue with God? How could the whole convention argue with God?

Paul and Barnabas told of other new Christians who weren't Jews. If God kept leading "strangers" into the group, how could the church contradict God?

Finally James, another one of the early church administrators, realized that the Divine Invisible Being was doing His job. The angel, the dream, the miracles, and the controversy in the church were all part of His message.

So James got up and spoke. "*It seemed good to the Holy Ghost*, and to us, to lay no greater burden than these necessary things" (Acts 15:28, emphasis added). James heard the Holy Spirit through all those events. Here he tells us how to hear the Divine Ghost for ourselves. We don't get heaven's message instantly; we get it eventually.

It took the Holy Spirit several years, and many miracles, before the Christian church understood Him. How long will it take before you and I get the point?

Whether the Divine Invisible Being is telling us to overcome intolerance or some other problem, the question to us is: are we listening? Certainly George Müller was listening when he opened orphanages in England, helping thousands of children. [29] Certainly Robert Moffat was listening when he gave his life for thousands of Africans who were living in painful conditions. [30] Certainly William Wilberforce was listening when he fought so strongly against slavery in England. [31]

How Do We Know We Heard?

How do you and I recognize the voice of the Divine Invisible Being? How do we distinguish His voice from all the other impressions and messages that come to us? The Bible is for exactly this. The Bible does not tell us what to do about our present lives. The Bible wasn't written about our world today. [32] It describes different times and different places. The Bible tells us what the Divine Invisible Being told others to do in those other times and places so long ago, and we can depend on the consistency of that same Invisible Being. He never changes. He never contradicts Himself (see Malachi 3:6; Hebrew 13:8) The advice He gave to mankind in the past is just as valid today as it was centuries ago. We can count on His advice to us as being consistent with His advice back then.

Consistency with the character of God as it is described in the Bible is the most accurate and best way to discern the voice of God in our personal lives and circumstances today. Whatever is in harmony with the will of God revealed in those sacred histories is valid for us today. Whatever disagrees with the messages brought to light in those same histories comes from some other voice than God.

There are other ways to recognize the voice of God as well. I personally suspect the Divine Invisible Being is speaking when the idea I get is too wise or too noble to come from another source. I recognize His voice when the idea I receive is contrary to what I want, and it turns out to be what I really need. I recognize the voice of God when I find the answer to a particular question more complete and satisfactory than I could ever expect or think to ask (see Ephesians 3:20). I recognize the voice of God when life keeps repeating the same lesson over and over to me until I understand it. In every instance in which I think I have heard the message of God, that impression is confirmed or refuted by a comparison with the character of God as mentioned previously.

Never have I claimed to hear the voice of the Invisible Being perfectly. There is always the chance that I have misunderstood Him. Therefore, I always need the humility to question how well I understood Him. Humility does not mean that I question whether or not He communicated. It only means that I question how well I have perceived His communication and recognize that my perception about His communication is something that can change.

What If I Can't Hear God?

Some of us have a harder time hearing the voice of God than others. Most of our trouble with hearing His voice comes from just a couple of reasons. One common reason is pain. When we hurt, that pain interferes with our hearing the communication of God.

Many of us have been hurt by other humans. Thus, we have scabs built up in our souls. We are angry and defensive. We cannot hear much because we are so wounded that we don't sense ideas when we are exposed to them. We often cannot hear other people. The words reach our ears, but the meaning of those words skips our heart. Hurt is one of the best earplugs our hearts could ever find.

Insecurity also closes us off to much of what surrounds us. It drowns out the music of the soul. We have trouble trusting a God we cannot see when we feel that we are hurt by the people we can see.

We look for comfort in the people we know even when that security is riskier than trusting the God we do not know. We choose the hurt we are accustomed to over the voice of God that is ultimately safe but currently unfamiliar.

Others of us don't hear the voice of God because He doesn't give us what we want. I liken this notion to a poor analogy I once encountered. A two-year-old boy saw two bright, shiny bottles in his parents' garage, so he wanted them. His parents kindly but firmly refused to give them to him. The little boy got angry. He wanted those two bottles that were out of his reach, and he wanted them now. The little fellow could not understand why dad wouldn't give him bleach and cyanide. So he treated his father very rudely for not giving him what he wanted. God doesn't give us the poisons in life that we ask for, and we get mad.

On the other hand, it is like the girl who asked dad for a car at the age of four. Dad had already purchased a rare vintage car and had it waiting for her. For her fifth birthday he gave her the car keys, but he didn't give her a key to the garage where her pretty car was parked. She had to grow up first. Just like the little girl, we have to grow up many times before God gives us what we ask for and need. We often find that patience with God is hard. In the hindsight of both cases, we are grateful for God's wisdom. Still, it is much harder to trust Him up front.

When we are willing to let go of our hurt and our insecurities, we can hear God. When we are willing to be patient until we are mature enough for what we ask, we can hear God. When we are willing to open ourselves to learn the lessons that keep repeating themselves so mysteriously in our lives, we can hear God. When we listen in the stillness of the soul, God will speak. We will know it is God because it is the same voice that has been speaking for thousands of years. It is the same voice the Bible tells us about so well.

Then we can receive the greatest human experience possible. It is the most satisfying event to ever occur. Our mindset and lifestyle change. Worry and anxiety run away from us. Contentment surrounds and fills us. We suddenly find ourselves the happiest and most satisfied we've ever been. We are not suddenly geniuses or forever faultless. We have only started a better way of life. There is a lot to learn, but we are learning, and that is exhilarating.

We have never tried our best in life until we have asked God to help us. When we are willing to ask Him, He will move rocks that are in our way. Asking an invisible God is difficult for us to do, but when we stop to listen, we can hear the voice of God in the stillness of our souls. That voice is consistent with the stories and teachings of the Bible. That voice repeats itself over and over again to us. That voice guides us to joy and contentment. That voice comforts and strengthens us through pain. That voice is patient with our misunderstandings, firm with our faults, and loving with our vulnerabilities. That voice is God talking to us. We may not understand Him perfectly. We may be more like babies taking their first wobbly steps than mature adults who can run or even walk on stilts. We may be more like two-year-olds asking silly questions than retiring scientists respected the world over for their knowledge and experience. Still, we can trust that *He* is talking to us.

Knowing that God hears us and talks with us, we can ask Him for His help. Only then we can *do* our very best. We can *live* our best. Asking the Wisest Being in the Universe for wisdom, strength, and courage, is satisfying. Seeing personal, family, and community problems resolved by ways we could never imagine, is thrilling. Always having a Resource to help us improve our own attitudes and perspectives is fulfilling. We may find God in the hardest moments of life. But we reach the best moments of human existence, the deepest and strongest joys we are capable of perceiving, under His nurturing guidance. I have yet to find an end to the glory that surrounds me as I open myself up to the Divine Invisible Being .We can *be* our best—this experience is heavenly. In fact, *it is heaven,* or at least it is part of experiencing heaven. For heaven begins by reaching out and accepting God and depending on Him.

Let's find the rest of heaven in the next two chapters.

Chapter 4
A HEAVENLY BATTLE

Heaven Never Agrees with Evil

Peace and evil cannot coexist. You and I will never find the peaceful society we inwardly desire until the existence of evil has been overcome. To have peace is not freedom from conflict; it is victory over everything that destroys peace. The fight will go on between peace and evil until one of the two is victorious. Who is responsible for this victory?

There are three predominant answers in our society today. One idea is that *our society* is responsible for overcoming evil. The battle is a team effort. Evil, with all of its consequences, and personal character, with all of its failings, are considered community "problems." "Educated" people provide a consensus of what is acceptable and what is unacceptable behavior. Every person is expected to meet this consensus.

Evil is blamed on a lack of resources or on the "backward thinking" of individuals who do not cooperate fast enough with community plans and community beliefs. People who perpetrate individual evil acts are promptly shamed and isolated from society. Character issues are otherwise considered the result of inheritance or circumstance and are not considered the result of personal mistakes or the breakdown of personal responsibility.

The solution to evil in this way of thinking is conformity to the community. Do what the experts direct. Fall in line with the powerful leaders of ideas, and the world will be safe and wonderful.

Those who suffer the consequences of evil must be helped by the community in the exact way the community determines is best. If someone is hungry, thirsty, without shelter, friendless, lacking medical treatment, without sufficient entertainment, or otherwise suffering from the effects of evil, the solution is for the community to offer yet another program to give the sufferer what they need. Poverty, homelessness, and social inferiority are all the fault of everyone for not being more compassionate. Compassion is primarily demonstrated by channeling resources through ever more powerful (and occasionally ever less accountable) institutions. This way of thinking sees evil as a community problem that will be solved by community cooperation.

Another idea is that the responsibility is more personal. Those who believe this idea speak of personal success, personal failure, personal generosity, and personal contribution. Those who commit evil acts are expected to be held personally accountable for the negative consequences of their actions. Those who suffer the consequences of the evil that exists in this world are to be privately helped by those who can help the sufferer to thrive, not just survive.

Unfortunately, those who see the solution to evil as a community project can be very thoughtless concerning the dignity, the needs, and the values of the individual. Furthermore, those who see the solution to evil as individual can become so focused on their own individual successes that they forget the necessity of stopping evil and providing for its victims in those around them.

Both of these viewpoints agree on one idea. There is one area of human life that people will never cede to the genius of public control: aesthetics. We may consult the opinions and guidance of others. We may study our own appearance carefully or ignore it and hope others don't suffer too much shock from what they see. But we are not interested in giving up the possibility of choosing how we look on the outside. Rich and poor, liberal and conservative, generous and stingy all consider their personal appearance to be their own personal responsibility. Also, outside of some zoning restrictions in some places, people of today widely expect individuals to be personally responsible for their choices in the appearance of their own homes and vehicles. We understand individual accountability in matters of appearance.

We expect the individual to be accountable for the exterior presentation of his or her body and belongings. Why do we care so little about who we are on the inside? There is an old expression: "Not everyone was given a beautiful face; but everyone can offer a friendly face."[33] Our external appearance is only partially inside of our control. We live with the face we were given and the resources available to us, but our characters are more fully under our control. We can design our own internal beauty. We can choose to be "friendly." The legacy of our ancestors influences us, but we can transcend that legacy if we so choose.

Character is not handed out randomly. It is not a reward given away to good people. It cannot be purchased. It is the result of thousands of choices repeated over and over again. It is the sum of the habits we choose for ourselves. We cannot get it secondhand. Character only works when it is individually chosen.

Firmness, patience, determination, respect, honor, sympathy, kindness, a sense of fairness, and a commitment to justice are not things we can take off in the evening and put back on in the morning. They are there all the time, or they are not there at all. We may sometimes fake them, but eventually our inner broken characters will spill out of the best kept defenses. These qualities are easier for some of us and more challenging for others. Nevertheless, we are all more responsible for who we are than for how we look.

We cannot live a life of peace and decency on borrowed charm. Why, then, do we expect everyone else to ignore our impatience, rudeness, injustice, and our lack of kindness, determination, respect, firmness, and sympathy? Why do we ignore our characters or outsource the development of them to someone else? We are personally responsible for the victory over atrocity because there is no other way for us to be fit to be part of any heaven.

We can help hold each other accountable for our character, but no one else can form that character for us. We can encourage and support each other, but we cannot remake each other.

Can't we share this responsibility with God? Isn't He the One who will overcome all evil and provide peace in its place? This is the third idea: God is responsible for conquering evil.

Who brought evil into our world? God did not. Humans did. Here it is very tempting to only blame our ancestors. But if the only injustice ever committed in our world was Adam and Eve stealing a snack, our lives would be a lot better off than they are now. If we humans never committed another evil act on the globe, the consequences of our ancestors' transgressions would be a lot easier to address. We who are alive today are the ones who continue the evil introduced by our ancestors. We who are alive today are the cause of every evil action that occurs on this planet while it is "under our watch." We who are alive right now are responsible for the occurrence of the evil that is happening. Do not blame God or our ancestors or even the devil for what *we* choose to do now!

Can't we just make the mess and then let God clean it up? Won't God take care of the consequences of our mistakes just like some parents pick up dropped toys behind their children? Isn't the real heaven in the future filled with people with "hearts of gold" walking on streets of gold after God finishes making them perfectly good? Won't we all be as contented and moral as the heavenly angels when God does all the dirty work for us and we can then all live happily ever after?

No! God is not some sort of moral tyrant who will sweep in and make evil a thing of the past. He won't get rid of evil just to make heaven for all us. Let us ask the men who lived with God over 2,000 years ago. Somehow walking beside Jesus, helping Jesus distribute miraculously multiplied bread to 4,000 men, and watching Jesus heal the helpless taught the disciples that Jesus was deeply concerned with the presence and the consequences of evil in the world of their day. Jesus faced it head on. Watching Jesus chase evil (and the religious leaders in its grip) out of the temple and hearing Him rebuke those same religious leaders who abused power convinced the disciples that He was going to overcome evil on earth.

After watching Jesus and listening to Him, Peter put his certainty of what Jesus will do with evil in the future this way: "The day of the Lord will come as a thief in the night; in the which the heavens shall pass away with a great noise, and the elements shall melt with fervent heat, the earth also and the works [including the evil] that are therein shall be burned up" (2 Peter 3:10). It was absolutely clear to Peter that Jesus will completely destroy evil by burning it up in the universe's greatest bonfire. Peter also expected that this destruction of our globe and of evil would be followed by "new heavens and a new earth, wherein dwelleth righteousness" (v. 13).

There we have it. Jesus is responsible for conquering evil. He will take care of it. We can sit back and wait on Him.

How long will we have to wait, though? It's been 2,000 years since Peter told his readers that Jesus would take care of evil, and every morning since Peter wrote those words, the sun still comes up on another day just like every other day. The world still goes round without melting in a big fire. Peter anticipated our secular skepticism. "So what's happened to the promise of [Jesus'] Coming? Our ancestors are dead and buried, and everything's going on just as it has from the first day of creation. Nothing's changed" (v. 4 *The Message*).

Peter knew His Friend and Teacher and Savior. He had watched Jesus for so long that he began to understand His character. He explained that Jesus was and is waiting to abolish evil. He is waiting not because He doesn't care or because He wants evil to exist; He is waiting to give us a chance to overcome evil. He is "not willing that *any* should perish, but that all should come to repentance" (v. 9, emphasis added). Peter only echoed the words of Jesus as quoted centuries earlier by Ezekiel.

> "Repent and turn from all your transgressions, lest iniquity be your ruin. Cast away from you all the transgressions which you have committed against me, and get yourselves a new heart and a new spirit! Why will you die, O house of Israel? For I have no pleasure in the death of any one, says the Lord God; so turn, and live" (Ezekiel 18:30-32, RSV).

Jesus is so compassionate that He will not destroy evil until you and I are willing to overcome it (or we are so committed to our nefarious behavior that there is no hope of rescuing us). [34] He is patient with us, waiting for us to take responsibility for the evil we cause and repent. There is nothing tyrannical about Jesus. He suffers through every evil committed, waiting on us.

We are tempted to look at God with impatience because He has not taken care of the problem of evil already. Peter knew God intimately, and he saw the continued existence of evil as a condition permitted only because of God's patience with us. Peter saw God's willingness to do for us whatever we will accept to support us and help us to conquer evil, but He *never forces us to take something better than what we have chosen*. This man that knew God best saw His compassion in refusing to force on us a world without evil that we have not chosen. He saw God's painful nobility in leaving to us the battle against what we have caused. Nowhere does God ever promise to force peace on us. He is not going to ever change us unless we are willing to accept His help. We need to stop waiting around for God to suddenly abolish evil and thereby become the tyrant He will never be.

Peter saw the continuation of crime and heartbreak today not as God's fault, but rather as His virtue. He saw Jesus demonstrating a divine longsuffering, as His heart continues to ache with the pain we cause each other. Peter saw Jesus grieved as He stands by us ignored and insulted, all the while offering us the solution to all evil. Jesus longs for us to take our own personal responsibility for what we contribute to the global existence of evil and ask for His help to stop making monthly, daily, and sometimes hourly payments of our own malice, hatred, and nefariousness.

Maybe you are thinking of how weak and helpless you and I are to fight against evil. We are incapable of victory without God, but He will not impose victory without mankind. He needs our choice, and we need His power, wisdom, love, justice, and compassion. Conquering what is wrong in our world is a battle that requires the closest teamwork between God and each one of us.

Nevertheless, this view of God is not one that everyone shares today. In spite of Jesus' suffering and compassion, many people are afraid of God, of the Bible, and even of churches today. They fear that God or the Bible or the church is some sort of tyrant going around enforcing morality, nobility, and beautiful characters in the present. Some churches and some church people have done this and worse. No matter how much they pretend, these people are not of God. God does not force.

Our fear says volumes about those of us who are fearful. On one hand, we do not want to take personal responsibility for the evil we cause and overcome it. We long to avoid moral responsibility. On the other, we do not want God to force us to say or do anything. We do not want Him to overcome evil by doing it for us without our choice. Our fears expose us to our own love/hate relationship with evil. We want others to overcome evil, but we are afraid to give up our own internal ugliness.

Of course, we do not admit this in public. No one writes articles or prepares documentaries on the moral irresponsibility of the average person. We don't talk about being afraid of God because He might make us be kinder or more firm, more compassionate or more organized. We all tell ourselves that we are respectable people. We are civilized and refined. Barbarism has gone the way of dinosaurs. We are sure that we have outgrown barbaric behavior by our own human ability to overcome malice and malevolence.

Are we as far away from being uncivil as we boast that we are? Why don't we call barbaric behavior today by what it is—barbarism? Can we be smug that humanity has moved past terrible behavior? Has our humanistic attempt to conquer malice, contempt, and malevolence worked?

Some suggest that disposing of religion will make us more civilized and well-behaved citizens, but we have tried this. For example, the former Union of Soviet Socialist Republics suppressed religion for decades. During these years of suppression, atheistic leaders freely and barbarically killed a wide variety of those who doubted or disagreed with them politically or otherwise. [35] An absence of religion never made them, or any of the other large, atheistic governments, more civilized.

Others propose that a system for letting the majority rule will make us civilized, but the majority is not always right or kind. Many of the most barbaric acts of the last few centuries have had the support of the majority. The injustices committed against the Native Americans were done by a democracy. [36] Importing thousands of Africans against their will and forcing them into slavery was done by the greatest of democracies. [37] The extermination of millions of Jews and others ordered by Adolf Hitler was supported by a majority, even if they were not a democracy. [38] In each of these moments of history the minority needed to be heard and respected. Instead, the majority supported various cruelties, and many people perpetrated acts of total barbarism.

Others propose that education makes us civilized. The facts just noted about World War II Germany demonstrate that education and intellect and a rule supported by the majority do not protect humanity from barbaric acts of murdering minorities.

The difference between civilized and barbaric behavior is not how well we are groomed or how sophisticated our ideas are or how popular our personalities are. Beauty and intelligence and charm do not make us decent. We eradicate barbarity by overcoming any hint of evil in ourselves. The difference between civil and uncivil behavior is the difference between those who—with God's help to move their personal rocks—take responsibility for their own characters and those who refuse to fight the least glimmer of evil in themselves.

Fighting the evil in our own characters is a war. This war against atrocity is different than any other war we have ever seen or thought about, for heaven is not hostile toward people. Jesus fought this war in front of our ancestors by doing battle against immorality when it tempted Him and when it conquered those around Him. He demonstrated that this war is personal; it is internal, not external. It fights against actions and thoughts by individuals taking responsibility for their own behavior and choosing to change their own character with the help of the Divine.

The goal of the internal war for our minds is to make us the most peaceful people alive in a troubled world, for when we are victorious over every evil thought and impulse inside ourselves, we will have no evil thoughts left for doing evil outside of ourselves. [39] Heaven exists where there is a group of people who never do a single evil act nor say an evil word.

The evil inside of our own thoughts and characters are the stones [40] that we cannot seem to move out of our way today. The impatience with our families, the slights to our colleagues, the dishonesty with ourselves seem hopelessly lodged in the way of our daily lives. The greater injustices of theft and murder and many more terrible actions seem impossible to prevent. Our world would truly be a good place if every one of us conquered evil, no matter how insignificant it seems. We need the help of God to give wisdom and power to our determination to resist and overcome evil. We need to personally take responsibility for our own characters and influences and make sure that neither provides the least room for evil in our world today. For too long we have used the existence of other people's evil actions to ignore and distract ourselves from our own contributions toward evil. [41]

Today, one of the most difficult tasks we face as humans is to identify and conquer the evil that we are individually and collectively responsible for bringing to existence in the world around us. How do we define this war? How do we nourish personal responsibility for personal morality? What tools do we use in fighting? What are the rules for engagement? How can we fight evil *without becoming the evil we fight*? How can we achieve results in the last human frontier to be conquered: our individual and collective human characters?

What is clear from the dusty pages of history is that the battle must be fought against evil, for evil will never tolerate competition. Evil will ruin anything that does not conquer it. The essence of evil is its dedication to the unnecessary harm and eventual destruction of ourselves and anyone else it can touch. Maybe the same pages of history that tell us the battle against evil is necessary can guide us in how to win the war.

Rwanda currently faces a moral dilemma that is the direct result of the evil the country experienced. As many of us are aware, hundreds of thousands of people were killed in the genocide of 1994. [42] There is nothing heavenly in the stories of that war. Friends and extended family members became enemies. Neighbors killed each other. The murders were over who would control the country and the neighborhoods. They were based on ethnic heritage and destroyed thousands of men, women, and children who were no threat to anyone.

What do you do with so large a percentage of the population who are guilty of murder? Especially when the criminals are almost exclusively from one ethnicity, and the grieving families of the victims are from another ethnicity? How do you bring justice without committing reverse genocide?

Mukahirwa Stephanie knows the moral dilemma intimately. On the evening of Friday, April 8, 1994, Mrs. Stephanie was attending a church service. On this day after the genocide started, there was still much confusion and uncertainty. Many had no idea what was beginning to happen.

Following the church service, some of the church members stood up and locked the doors. They announced that nobody could go out and that all Tutsis were enemies of the country and of the church.

Mrs. Stephanie and the others stayed in the church that night. They didn't know what else to do. In the morning, Hutu soldiers arrived and ordered them to put down whatever they had. The only thing these church members had were Bibles. Certainly nothing that made them dangerous was in their hands. Their only "crime" was that some of them were a little taller than the Hutu soldiers.

The soldiers then ordered all the people to go outside, one by one, and lie on the ground. The machetes, spears, and guns in the hands of the soldiers didn't leave room to disobey or even disagree. After everyone was outside, the soldiers separated those who looked like Hutus from those who looked like Tutsis. The Tutsi people were ordered over toward the outhouse. Then the soldiers began firing. Many died on the spot. Any that were missed by the bullets were shoved into the cesspool to die by drowning in urine and feces.

Mrs. Stephanie survived down in that hole and finally escaped to a hospital where some kind Hutus hid her in various places until the killing stopped. After the war, Mrs. Stephanie found her daughter, Chantal. She grieved for her husband and son, whom she couldn't find.

Several years later, Pastor John Bosco invited Mrs. Stephanie to visit another church with him. After the service, John told her that someone wanted to talk with her. He also told her that this person was involved in killing her husband and son.

She found the possibility of meeting with this person terribly difficult. She knew that she was free to leave. She also sensed that she needed to stay. She chose to sit face to face with Evaliste. Mrs. Stephanie's body shook with pain and nervousness as Evaliste admitted to murdering her closest family. He told of the agony it had caused him. He took responsibility by admitting that it was evil to do what he did and that he had been more like a crazy animal than a human being when he did it. Then he asked for her forgiveness. He had asked for this meeting with Mrs. Stephanie because he wanted to apologize to her.

How do you forgive a monster? She struggled with how to respond to his request for forgiveness. She waited, filled with grief and anger. It was a painful moment for both of them. Could she forgive the man who had murdered her family? Could she let go of her anger toward the one who had caused her years of suffering in the form of loneliness and financial struggle? Certainly killing Evaliste would not solve the problem of ethnic killing in Rwanda. If Mrs. Stephanie killed Evaliste, it would only be to reverse sides in the perpetual cycle of ethnic cleansing. It would be just another act of genocide, even if he deserved to die. She determined to stop the cycle of death. Slowly she reached out her hand to Evaliste and said, "I forgive you."

Mrs. Stephanie wrote afterward, "I felt a great burden falling off my heart when I stretched out my hand … Since that day, I have been at peace with the Lord. I don't keep any resentment or bitterness in my heart. The Holy Spirit helped me to overcome this great trauma in my life." [43]

Her story may be difficult or troubling to some of us. Would we be willing to forgive the person who murdered those whom we love? Could we do it when they admitted their guilt and asked for forgiveness? Would it take us a day, a week, a year, a lifetime?

What is the alternative? Were Tutsis to commit genocide against Hutus and then Hutus against Tutsis and then Tutsis against Hutus, nothing would be accomplished but the killing off of the human race in Rwanda. In places where terrible evils have occurred, humanity is confronted with the necessity of forgiveness. In Rwanda, there were only two options: relentlessly continue committing genocide back and forth between the two peoples or find a way to reconcile with those who have done the evil.

Fundamentally, evil will never be conquered around this globe while we use evil to fight evil. Violence and prison and treaty may quarantine malevolence, but they do not abolish evil. Evil is conquered only by reconciliation between the one responsible for it and the one who suffers the consequence of it. This reconciliation occurs only when there is forgiveness. The Rwandans who carry firewood and water for the grieving family members of the victims of their own machetes are overcoming evil. When a former criminal and the family of his deceased victim can pray and laugh and work together, evil is conquered.

What do you and I believe about forgiveness anyway? Most of us have never confronted the opportunity to forgive someone for causing us such terrible suffering the way that Mrs. Stephanie did. However, every one of us has been injured by those around us at some moment in our lives. All of us have had the opportunity and need to forgive. Unfortunately, we have also experienced the need to ask for forgiveness.

What we know from the personal experience of those who have forgiven is that forgiveness does as much or more for the one who offers it as it does for the one who receives it. Mrs. Stephanie immediately identified the benefits for her of forgiving Evaliste. "I have been at peace; I don't keep any resentment or bitterness in my heart; The Holy Spirit helped me to overcome this great trauma in my life." We who have been wronged by our family members, friends, and strangers need these benefits of forgiveness. We need the peace and freedom from bitterness, anger, and anxiety that comes with offering forgiveness. But there is more to forgiveness than just helping ourselves.

Our society does not have a consensus on forgiveness. Some of us consider it optional. For many of us, it is simply a way to change ourselves so that we no longer brood over the injuries we have experienced. We see forgiveness as a solo experience, aimed at making life easier for *me*. We talk of forgiving those who are dead and those who do not have any communication with us. We talk of forgiving those who refuse to admit that they hurt us and those who never ask for our forgiveness.

All of this talk about forgiveness is easier (not that it is easy) when we are discussing the mistakes that we make toward each other from day to day. It is much more difficult when we talk about malicious behavior. The man who drinks before going home to beat and yell obscenities at his family; the drug addict who puts money into feeding his addiction instead of housing, clothing, and even feeding his live-in girlfriend and her babies; the colleague at work who systematically spreads rumors to undermine your career all make forgiveness a more difficult subject. Can we risk forgiving those who perpetrate evil?

Many Rwandans have found the answer to be "yes." Forgiveness was the best tool against evil that was available for Mrs. Stephanie to use with Evaliste that was not an act of evil in itself. Forgiveness is the only way for her fellow Rwandans to live with that many criminals among them. Forgiveness is the best way to stop evil.

Forgiveness is one of the principal tools heaven uses to battle against evil. It is a tool that is often misunderstood and abused. It is also taken advantage of very often. Nevertheless, as Mrs. Stephanie discovered, it is powerful. This may be a different way to look at forgiveness and a different meaning of the very word "forgiveness" than we are accustomed to using.

Christianity has been too tolerant of a false concept of forgiveness. The idea has gone about that forgiveness does not eradicate evil; it only stops us from some of the pain we experience that is brought on by evil. We hear that forgiveness makes us able to endure the evil in this world a little easier, but it really does nothing to stop evil in its tracks. This makes forgiveness into an act that breaks down order and dignity in society by refusing to hold accountable those who commit evil acts among us. It makes forgiveness a sign of weakness and an act of cowardice. This idea of forgiveness is a falsehood. Forgiveness may give up the demand for full vengeance, [44] but it is still willing and able to hold the perpetrator accountable. Forgiveness is not a sign of weakness. It is proof of power—divine power manifested in human action. A Bible story is enough to demonstrate that to receive forgiveness is a life-changing experience.

Jesus was a guest of Simon, an important Jew (Mark 14:3–9; Luke 7:36–50). Simon failed to show Jesus the most common of courtesies, such as welcoming Him at His arrival with the culturally common kiss and providing for Jesus' comfort by the customary washing of His feet. Yet another guest, possibly uninvited and unwanted—one of the town's "second-class" citizens—did both for Jesus without being asked. Why did this "sinner" risk the social stigma of volunteering to do what Simon neglected? Jesus stated that her love for Him demonstrated her experience of forgiveness, and Simon's cold and calloused welcome of Jesus occurred because he was not forgiven (Luke 7:47). [45]

Forgiveness is the choice to hold someone accountable for their evil actions while not requiring them to experience all the consequences of what they have done. It is an act, the ultimate act, of grace. [46]

God has never given us forgiveness as long as we *insist* on repeating the wrong. [47] The Bible connects confession, forgiveness, and being made innocent. "*If we confess our sins, He is faithful and just to forgive us our sins, and to cleanse us from all unrighteousness*" (1 John 1:9). Receiving forgiveness and being reconciled with God is a treasure that is "bought" by "selling all that" we "have" (Matthew 13:44–46). In practical life Peter, the disciple, experienced this surrender of giving up all he had as part of his moment of finding forgiveness. However, selling all that he had and "buying" heaven never included the exchange of money. The only thing he could offer God in his moment of remorse was his own ugly history, his own moral faultiness. When the rooster crowed, Peter "went out, and wept bitterly" (Matthew 26:75). Godly sorrow or deep remorse that gives up our own personal histories and our characters with all their flaws to God in turn produces repentance. This remorse includes increased carefulness or diligence, a holy determination to be clear of all guilt, anger at past actions of injustice, a vehement desire or longing for restoration, and zeal to do differently (see 2 Corinthians 7:10–12). This forgiveness includes the order "Go, and sin no more" (John 8:11). [48] The act of forgiveness is life-changing. God changes our behavior as He forgives us. Forgiveness has never taken place if we keep repeating the same offense, endlessly.

Many times we cheapen forgiveness with apologies we do not mean. We say we are sorry just to sound polite. After a while, our obvious lie becomes insulting. We say we regret hurting the other person, but we keep repeating what injures them. It becomes apparent that we do not have any regret at all. We expect them to suffer and smile while we whitewash our insincerity with a trite apology. This may work with humans, but never expect God to put up with such hypocrisy. If you aren't actually filled with remorse and regret for treating Him ungratefully and insultingly, don't lie to Him with apologies you don't mean. Divine forgiveness is not a cute way to gain emotional security. It is not a way to maintain a dishonest relationship with a strictly honest God. It is reconciliation between we who have wronged God and the God whom we have wronged. It is the removal of every one of the morally irresponsible character traits that injure our relationship with God even as they injure us and other humans. Jesus plainly stated that the person who has been forgiven by Him loves Him (Luke 7:47). His concept of forgiveness is active and not passive.

There is a direct consequence to this active forgiveness. People who were previously dangerous become safe. The Hutu murderer is no longer a threat to Mrs. Stephanie. Mr. Evaliste has chosen to hold himself accountable for his own terrible actions. His own conscience and will (supported by the strength of God) keep him from repeating his own crime. She can forgive him because his sincere apology, supported by his actions, demonstrates that he is no longer a threat to her. Neither of them has forgotten that Evaliste's crime tore Mrs. Stephanie's husband and son from out of her life. The past cannot be undone. But they can be friends in the present. They can help each other in the present. They can build a relationship of mutual trust and respect in the present.

The power of forgiving others is in recognizing the enormity of the guilt, in recognizing the accountability of the perpetrator, and in recognizing that there is no more need to hold the perpetrator accountable when he or she has held him or herself accountable. Forgiveness is an act of deference to the perpetrator's new character. When the one who caused the injury realizes what he or she has done is wrong and goes to the victim with strong remorse, pleading for forgiveness and doing everything possible to make the matter right, the perpetrator becomes trustworthy again. We can now rest in the restored accountability and self-government of the former perpetrator. When I forgive, that forgiveness is a statement that I am willing to stop protecting myself from you. I do not have to protect myself anymore because you have demonstrated that you are in control of yourself. I can trust you to no longer hurt me. I will no longer hold you accountable for who you were because I accept you for who you have become.

Too often, we confuse *offering to forgive* with *forgiveness* itself. We can offer to forgive without any change in the other person. *Offering to forgive* is a change in ourselves so that we are *willing* to stop protecting ourselves from the other person. But forgiveness cannot be complete until the other person has taken responsibility for injuring us. That other person has to demonstrate that he or she is taking responsibility by apologizing and making right, as far as possible, his or her wrongdoing. If we forgive and restore without this apology and restitution, we open ourselves to being abused. [49] In asking us to seek God's forgiveness and to forgive each other, God is not asking us to open ourselves up to abuse. Just because God does not use abuse to stop abuse does not mean that He tolerates abuse. The life work of Jesus 2,000 years ago was to stop the spiritual abuse of the clergy of that time. It was the work of stopping their abuse that drove the clergy to hate and finally kill Him. Ending abuse was so important to Him that He sacrificed His life to this cause. It is impossible for Him to teach that we should support and tolerate abuse when He died in the cause of ending it.

That is why the idea that God forgives us without any reconciliation with us is so contradictory to the message of Jesus. Today we hear a lot about grace and God's forgiveness. Grace is presented in a way that makes it sound like God doesn't care what we do or how we do it. As long as we chant His name or mumble an apology, He spontaneously makes any guilt vanish. We can still be cruel and do evil things, but we feel guilt-free because of God's "sleight of hand."

Essentially, this idea of grace is saying that God's forgiveness is a way for Him to "cook" the heavenly record books and make it look like we are innocent when we really just keep repeating the same injustices. We make God into a really tough Being who absorbs our endless abuse of Him. We accuse God of being "the heavenly liar," busy making up good lies to protect His buddies down here on planet Earth. [50]

These false perceptions present an unfair picture of God; they reveal a great deal of confusion in us about God's actual character. These untruths are an attempt to turn forgiveness into a perception that God sees evil and merely "shrugs His shoulders," so to speak. He permits evil and ignores guilt just so long as the perpetrator sends Him a brief prayer. It is amazing that we humans would even think of insulting God by talking about Him not taking evil seriously. But any discussion of grace that does not involve that grace working out a change in forgiven humanity is nothing more than a claim that God does not take evil seriously at all. [51]

This idea that God can't be bothered by evil (what an insult to Him!) is essentially saying that God embraces and accepts it. This falsehood distracts from the truth that God's forgiveness *does not accommodate* evil; it is a fundamental tool in *overcoming* and *conquering* it. God offers His forgiveness and grace to every human, and the forgiveness and grace that He offers cost Him more than we could ever repay Him. It cost Him everything. Let us add up a part of the cost to God of offering us forgiveness.

God suffers as He watches evil unfold across the entire history of this planet. God suffers with each injury any human experiences because He wants to prevent that injury and comfort every sufferer. God also knows that it would spoil the lesson if He did what He wanted and moved ahead faster than we could understand and accept. Jesus suffered the humiliation of becoming one of us, His creatures, when we were at our most inglorious moment of existence. The Father and the Holy Ghost suffered while supporting Jesus in the hardest possible "mission" God could undertake. Then They suffered the agony of watching Jesus suffer the pain and indignity of the cross. Jesus endured the punishment of a terrible criminal by the death penalty. Jesus' pain continues due to our hatred, carelessness, and injustice, all of which He hates. The ache of the Father, Son, and the Holy Ghost is prolonged as they bear with our ingratitude when we throw Their grace away. Every step God has taken in offering His grace to humans has cost God and cost Him dearly. Providing grace to us has been and continues to be the most heartrending experience our marvelous God has ever undergone.

We have hurt God, and He has chosen the difficult (even for Him) course of offering us forgiveness despite our lack of gratitude. Grace and forgiveness are not cheap or convenient for God.

God offers these, the most expensive gifts in the universe, to those who accept them by their attitude of a willingness to let go of evil.

Jesus talks of "any one" that "is willing to do His will..." (John 7:16 *Weymouth New Testament*). As we said before, "If we confess our sins, He is faithful and just to forgive us our sins, and to cleans us from all unrighteousness" (1 John 1:9). David summarizes experiencing these gifts of grace and forgiveness. "I acknowledge my sin unto thee, and mine iniquity have I not hid. I said, I will confess my transgressions unto the Lord; and thou forgavest the iniquity of my sin" (Psalm 32:5).

We say that grace is free. This is true. It is free, for it would not be grace if we ever had to pay for it. If we could offer enough prayers to pay for God's help and blessing, salvation would be a business deal. We could negotiate with God and make a contract. "I'll do 1,975 kindnesses for others this year and throw in church attendance for good measure. You, God, will bless me in whatever way I ask." Salvation would then become a commercial business that we could manipulate. These "commercialized" blessings would no longer be equally available to each human being. Some of us would hoard our blessings and others would struggle endlessly to get just a little.

Salvation, however, is not an industry. Salvation is an act of goodwill provided by God, which we can never pay for by any action or word we might offer. Like other gifts, it is not earned; salvation is accepted.

That same grace is not free from any cost. It never was. As noted earlier, every offer of grace cost God dearly. Today we have made His suffering too cheap by making His grace too cheap. When we ignore the trail of tears that God travels to reach each sinner, we insult God. The cross is only a single instance of the sorrow and hardship that grace costs God every day. God mercifully puts up with insults and snubs. God looks past rejection and hostility. He knows the glorious, thriving, contented person each of us would be if we were not wounded and stunted by evil. Saving each one of us is a painful act for God each time He does it.

Here we have a strong reason that heaven is always at war with evil. Every evil word or action is an insult to a gracious God and to the heaven He has provided. Evil is fundamentally an attack on good and on God. Insulting God and experiencing heaven are contradictions. The two can never go together.

The first words of Jesus to humanity after we first insulted Him in Eden were a promise to put the hatred of evil, enmity, into our hearts "I will put enmity between thee and the woman, and between thy seed and her seed; it shall bruise thy head, and thou shalt bruise his heel" (Genesis 3:15). Enmity: hatred or hostility. That is a strong word.

Hatred is exactly what Paul describes. "For that which I do I allow not: for what I would, that do I not; but what I hate, that do I." Romans 7:15. Different translations provide for a more precise grasp of this passage.

- "For what I am doing, I do not understand. For what I will to do, that I do not practice; but what I hate, that I do" (*New King James Version*).

- "For I understand not that that I work; for I do not the good thing that I will, but I do that evil thing that I hate" (*Wycliffe Bible*).

- "What I don't understand about myself is that I decide one way, but then I act another, doing things I absolutely despise" (*The Message*).

- "My own behaviour baffles me. For I find myself not doing what I really want to do but doing what I really loathe" (*J. B. Phillips New Testament*).

- "I do not understand my own actions. For I do not do what I want, but I do the very thing I hate" (RSV).

We hate evil because in Eden Jesus promised us to make us hate evil. Paul looked deep into his own heart and into our hearts and saw the hatred for evil that Jesus had promised, but hatred was not enough. Paul saw the same truth that we see in our world today. We need more than human help to cease from doing evil.

The struggle of our human existence ever since Jesus talked to our grandparents of long ago in Eden is our love-hate relationship with evil. We all hate the effects of evil. We all want those who do evil things to be held accountable, at least until we realize that we are just as much a guilty party as another person. Then we start offering justifications and excuses. We blame the circumstances, our inherited traits, the influence of others, or anything else that we think we can accuse. To sit humbly beside that Rwandan Hutu and voluntarily admit that we are to blame for the death of Mrs. Stephanie's husband and son is seemingly impossible.

How much better our world and our lives would be if we would just pull our attention out of the thousands of distractions and petty excuses of our lives and accept the forgiveness of God. How much better we would be if we never hurt God again!

Oh, how hard it is to let go of our own wrongs because we like them too much. When we talk about forgiveness, the size of the evil does not matter as much as our willingness to admit that we committed it. Try as we might, we can never justify doing evil. But often the size of the evil matters a lot when we suffer the injustice rather than being the perpetrator. In our eyes, murder is a greater harm than a petty insult. The size does not matter when we consider that we need to apologize and make right what we have done wrong. The size of the evil does not matter when we confess it to God; we just need to make the confession.

Part of our love-hate relationship with evil comes from our inability to conquer evil on our own. We are helpless in our struggle to overcome, so we start justifying why we cannot change. Jesus, on the other hand, demonstrated conclusively that evil can be rejected; it can be conquered because God gives power to anyone who is willing to be made willing. [52]

What do we mean by evil? Evil is any thought or action that unjustifiably injures a creature of God. When a surgeon cuts a patient open to remove a ruptured appendix, that cut is an injury. But it is a justifiable injury toward a higher goal. Evil is every *unjustifiable* injury. The old word for it is "sin" or "iniquity." We have forgotten the deep-rooted meaning of that theological word in our world today as we now use the word sin to mean things very different than evil. We jovially call eating chocolate a sin and mean that while indulging in it, we chastise ourselves for doing so.

When the Bible uses the word "sin," it is talking about evil. When the Bible calls us sinners, it means that all of us have had evil thoughts and have done evil actions. Thus, the Bible offers divine forgiveness as the way to eradicate evil. God offers to pardon us for the evil we have committed. He offers to change us from doing evil ever again. He offers to make us truly evil-free people. He offers us His forgiveness and grace. He offers this only if we are willing to let go of the evil already working inside of us to be changed by Him so that we no longer do evil.

If God forgave those people who refuse to be changed by Him, He would turn Himself into a "punching bag." We hurt Him; He forgives us. We hurt Him all over again; He forgives us. We hurt Him all over again. This concept of forgiveness essentially views God as so tough He can handle the pain and us as so cruel that we are endlessly hurting

God. But that is "all right" because we ask God to let us off the hook for our cruel actions. This concept is not one of a partnership with God to make us better. It is not one of overcoming evil. It is one of demanding that God let us bring Him perpetual hell. We just season His pain with the trite and intellectually meaningless "I'm sorry" every so often. This concept is not one of overcoming evil but of being evil, perpetually. It is a concept that is an insult to ourselves and an insult to God. We are better people than to lead such an intellectually dishonest life of perpetual abuse to Someone we love. [53] There is more than just our own responsibility for evil to justify a war against it. Heaven fights against evil because that evil is an attack upon that which is good. When our Benefactor is attacked, we consider that we are attacked also, for we identify with Him. We cannot tolerate the evil that produces a disgust for God and tries to trash Him and His goodness to all of us. What insults God insults us because we are God's friends. As we accept heaven, we fight evil because we sympathize with God.

Mothers are jealous for their children. Insult one of the cubs, and mama bear gets angry. Insult one of her children again, and you'd better run for your life. When husbands love their wives, they are jealous also. You can joke about anything around them, and they may or may not laugh. Joke about a man's wife in a way that is insulting, and he will not laugh. Instantly, you know that he is angry. Don't try to explain away anything at that point. It's better apologize quickly, or you know you've lost his respect and maybe his friendship.

We are confused humans, and we get jealous for each other. How much more should we be jealous for God? We cannot be jealous for God, however, and at the same time accept and accommodate evil. The two cannot possibly go together.

There is another reason heaven does not tolerate evil. The moment heaven would accommodate evil, it would cease to be heaven. Heaven must fight against evil because you cannot live with evil and accept it without becoming evil.

Kevin Carter carefully adjusted the lens on his camera prior to taking a picture that would shock the world. Collapsed on the Sudanese ground lay a helpless, starving child in a crumpled heap just a short distance from food and help. Hunger had left nothing much to cover the bones under the brown skin. A few feet behind the child sat a vulture, waiting for death to come before having its meal.

Carter later agonized over that picture. He was haunted by the realization that he had never helped the poor, dying child get away from the vulture and to the nearby camp where food was waiting even though journalists were told not to touch people like this child because they could easily transmit disease to these weakened and vulnerable individuals. Carter later told a friend, "I'm really, really sorry I didn't pick the child up." The memory so deeply disturbed him that it contributed to his choice to end his own life. He could not live with the fact that he had documented evil without fighting it. Since he was close enough to take that painful photo, did he face the moral imperative to help despite the counsel given? Can anyone call it justice when we see the results of evil and do nothing about it? Heaven would not be heaven if it were to observe evil and do nothing.

Truly, the existence of evil demands action to conquer it. Let us observe evil (and this includes the painful work of documenting and using those documents to expose evil). However, observing evil is not enough. One of the tools of heaven is to observe and expose evil while simultaneously *helping its victims*. In fact, helping those who are the victims of evil is often the greatest way to expose the evil itself. Evil will never completely win when we help those who suffer from its torture.

Another of the great tools of heaven used to encourage observation, documentation, and exposure of evil is to demonstrate nobility in the face of evil. Show yourself more decent and dignified than evil in a nonviolent manner. Show evil to exist by demonstrating a nobility that reveals the existing evil in contrast with it. This was the great tool used by Martin Luther King Jr.[54] and Mohandas Gandhi.[55] We too can quietly demonstrate courage in the face of fear and do things that will force the injustices others are committing out into the open where others can see these for the evil that they really are.

This peaceable tool was used by Jesus long before either of them when He came to provide freedom from evil in our world. He fought evil by being noble in the face of evil men.

Two thousand years ago, the church clergy were not seen as representatives of evil. The Sadducees and Pharisees were the epitome of morality in their own minds. They were perceived as moral men by thousands of church members. We learn the evil inside the secret corners of their hearts because Jesus exhibited behavior that was nobler. When the church administration wanted to stone the woman whom they had "caught" in adultery" (John 8:4), Jesus saw her humility and quietness. He saw that she wanted to be forgiven, not killed and forgotten. He gave her the very forgiveness that the church administration refused her (John 8:10, 11).

Jesus never openly tried to ruin the temple or the church, but He helped the people marginalized by the church. We see murder in the hearts of the contemporary church administration only because we see the absence of hatred in the words and actions of Jesus.

These are powerful tools in the war against evil: ask for forgiveness, offer forgiveness, help the injured, encourage observation, documentation, and exposure where necessary;[56] and show courage and humility in the face of evil. We use these tools against evil because we are at war. Heaven must fight against evil because evil must be overcome or surrendered to. Heaven must battle against evil because it sympathizes with God. This is all part of the war that is heaven. But there is more to the fight.

The Power of One Loss

If the weather is comfortable, if we have a good home, if we are surrounded by a safe and supportive community, if we have delicious food, and if our work is rewarding, then we feel close to heaven. On the other hand, if one of our family members or friends is murdered, we suddenly don't feel anywhere close to heaven anymore. Few of our circumstances changed: we have the same house, same car, same friends (minus one), same job, and same food. Yet when evil hurts us, we often let go of heaven instantly. It only takes *one* evil action to take peace, security, and heaven away from us; which is why we must oppose *all* evil. It is not enough to oppose some of evil or even most of evil. For evil will never live peaceably in society. It always brings heartache and suffering with it. Our war against evil must be thorough. For heaven or evil will win, but both cannot win. One or the other will conquer, but the two can never get along together.

Any concept of heaven that accommodates any evil would not protect us from the destruction that all evil causes. This loss demonstrates once again the fundamental truth that heaven and evil cannot live together. The goodness of heaven is always giving and healing and uplifting. The evil of hell is always taking and hurting and destroying. Heaven is always exonerating and cherishing and valuing. Hell is always accusing and denigrating and belittling. Heaven isn't heaven if it just accepts the destruction of hell without any fight. We would be too vulnerable. Heaven stands firmly, never wavering, for "Jesus Christ [is] the same yesterday, and to day, and for ever" (Hebrews 13:8). Would heaven accept and accommodate evil, it would soon cease to be heaven, for that accommodation would force it to abandon the truths that make it fair and secure and respectable. Jesus demonstrated heaven because he conquered evil.

A certain kind of intolerance is necessary for a healthy life—an intolerance of evil. This is one of the great difficulties of our era. Many people have asked, "Why can't all humans just get along?" This is a good question. Why do powerful people take advantage of the weak? Why do seemingly happy marriages devolve into divorce? Why are there scandals and worse at work? Why do nations fight? Why do suicide bombings take place? Why can't we all just get along?

Many explanations can be offered to answer these questions. The reality is that we don't all get along. And we generally blame someone else for this. When we take responsibility for our contribution to "not getting along," then we have to ask ourselves why we have done something that hurts another human being. All of us will tell why it is that we hurt the feelings or the heart of someone else. But underneath of all of our explanations is one simple truth: we exhibit the character of hell because we have not wholeheartedly taken up the war against the evil in ourselves. We injure others because we tolerate our own evil.

I do not mean that we have not taken up fighting the war against evil in others. Let us never confuse the fight against evil around us with the fight against evil in us, for the war against evil starts at home, inside me, with myself.

We find it so difficult to look internally at our own error and evil. We easily see evil in others. So why do we have the boldness to fight someone else's faults while we nourish our own? Why do we expect someone else to abandon their wrongs while we cling to ours like a toddler clings to his "security" blanket? We must ask ourselves the question Jesus asked: why are we working so hard to take a splinter out of someone else's eye when we cannot see clearly because we have more than a splinter in our own eye?[57] There are evils that we cannot credibly oppose because we have greater evil in our own characters than the evil we are opposing in another.[58] We live in an age of expected toleration. We are asked to tolerate everything and everyone. However, this toleration of evil is impossible. Let's examine a marked example.

A citizen of Europe advertised a few years ago that he had a strong desire to cannibalistically eat another human. He put out advertisements on the internet asking for a voluntary victim. And another man responded, willing to become the sacrifice. Should we tolerate this modern, educated cannibal's desire? Should we protect his right to do what he wants? Why doesn't his hunger to eat another human deserve protection?

The great argument we have used for decades, that whatever I want should be tolerated by everyone else, does not hold up to honest investigation. Human desire [59] is not a criterion for what should or should not be tolerated. Heaven is the criterion for determining what should be tolerated. Thus, anything that is in harmony with heaven should be tolerated. Anything that is evil should not.

We believe in the value of a human life, but that belief in the value of human life is not the majority view of our world. In our human history and in many of the places around the world to this day, we humans do not consider human life very precious at all. The commitment to value human life is a minority view on our planet. In fact, we ought to thank the Protestant churches of past centuries for our appreciation of the value of life today. It is in countries where Protestant churches were predominant and mentored the popular culture over the last few centuries that this appreciation for human life first became the dominant accepted view.

The modern discussion of toleration misses the truth that toleration is impossible without intolerance. We cannot be tolerant of suicide bombing as just another acceptable lifestyle. Cannibalism (no matter how much "pleasure" it brought this particular individual) is not just another way of life to tolerate. Not all lifestyles are equally justified. And human pleasure does not determine which lifestyles are justified and which are not. So long as there are ways of life that cannot coexist, intolerance is necessary. Those who want to murder and are comfortable with it cannot live with those who oppose it. One side or the other must be intolerant because those two lifestyles cannot live with each other tolerantly and both sides be safe. Selected intolerance is essential to toleration.

It is true that there has been far too much intolerance in the world. It is also true that much of the world's intolerance is based on greed, envy, and ignorance. Much of the intolerance in this world is evil. As technology allows us to travel rapidly and communicate instantly over long distances, we are able to see some of the injustice of our intolerance. This does not mean, however, that the answer is to be tolerant of any behavior and any idea. We can only be tolerant of all people when we are intolerant of any evil behavior that hurts those people. It is the rejection (with God's help) of evil that will make this world safe for everyone, including the most vulnerable. [60]

At the heart of all the problems of this world is a tolerance of evil. We would have a peaceful haven on earth if every person was completely intolerant of evil in themselves and in their sphere of influence by the help of the Divine Invisible Being. This is the simple truth that we humans have completely underestimated. By personally taking responsibility for my contribution to the vast sum of evil in our world and overcoming it, I am actually contributing to heaven here and now, on earth.

There is one more reason that evil must be fought. Were heaven to tolerate evil, it would perpetuate massive confusion. Actions and habits and attitudes that can never live together (as just discussed) would be seen as the same. Destroying life would be seen as equally important as saving it. Respecting someone else's private property would be seen by others as morally equivalent to taking it unjustly for ourselves. Honesty and dishonesty, integrity and criminality, kindness and cruelty would all just be alternative lifestyles. The sacrifice of life given by firefighters while saving people from a burning building would become the moral equivalent of the murders of a serial killer. Judgment would be suspended exactly where it is most needed. Instead of distinguishing between heaven and evil, we would come to consider those two opposites the same thing. We would then become the breeding ground for self-deception. For we have to practice self-deception in order to harmonize and accept things that are contradictory. It would take massive doses of self-deception to keep up the constant lie that there is no moral difference, no valuable distinction between what destroys life and what protects it.

That self-deception would then become its own kind of self-destruction. An internal lack of honesty is the greatest crime a human can commit. In deceiving ourselves, we prevent ourselves from ever being helped or educated.

There is a great difference between saying heaven is committed to the eradication of evil and saying that heaven never agrees with evil. "Eradicate" is an active word. "Agreement" can be active or passive. Probably every human on earth does not agree with the consequences of evil when those consequences hurt them or people they love. We are angry when innocent people get hurt, especially if we think we are the innocent one. Yet heaven does more than disagree with evil, it fights against evil and it has won and will win.

Fighting against evil requires more strength and courage than may be obvious. It is tougher to silently suffer and conquer any interna temptation to hate the one who is hurting you than it is to injure the other person in protecting yourself. Heaven is not soft or easy. It is intolerant of evil. That steadfast, determined intolerance of evil is the hardest challenge we ever face.

Evil Never Conquers Evil

Heaven is not a hopeless fight. It knows how to pick its fights to win the battle, and it knows what tools it can use. Intellect, authority, power, aggressiveness, and charm all succeed as tools of power and influence. But none of these are enough to overcome evil. The primary tool that heaven employs is love, for heaven wages war first and foremost with love. That love includes forgiveness, and when necessary, a thoughtful exposure of evil, especially by demonstrating nobility in the face of evil. "He will again have compassion on us, and will subdue our iniquities. You will cast all our sins into the depths of the sea" (Micah 7:19). Other tools that heaven uses include education, generosity, appreciation, and determination.

These great tools for attacking and overcoming evil allow us to fight without ever being evil, which is one of the greatest dangers we face. All of us instinctively want to oppose evil, yet all too often human nature fights the evil in others by committing evil. We fight the injustice of others by being unjust back to them. If they humiliate us, we humiliate them. If they hurt us, we hurt them. In the process, we have become the evil we hated. We create a downward cycle of evil that has no end.

We see this in suicide bombers. In their own minds, these people have valid concerns. They think that the injustices they fight against are very real, but the injustices they cause by murdering others mitigate any argument they wish to make. We cannot understand any concerns they may have (mixed in with many invalid and unreasonable matters no doubt) because they are using evil to fight against what they perceive to be evil.

It is impossible to ever conquer evil with evil. It is impossible to overcome someone else's hatred of you by hating them.

Heaven has the most powerful tools; they've already proven that they will win. But these tools win over the long run whereas evil is sometimes perceived to win at first. In fact, evil's temporary triumph is exactly what eventually undermines it, for then we begin to see it for what it is and to hate it.

Heaven's Success Depends on Its Soldiers

Heaven is as successful in its fight against evil as the people who have heaven in their souls. If we think that evil is winning, it is because we have let go of heaven and are content with the presence of evil instead of heaven. Here we must recognize that heaven has been betrayed by many of its advocates. Over and over, the soldiers of heaven have fought the battles of hell, used the tools of hell, and sown the seeds of hell. The soldiers of heaven must be distinguished from the servants of hell, who betray their own cause. We should never let the failure of the wayward soldiers distract us from heaven itself. Let us never honor their betrayal by falling for it.

Evil will be fully conquered one day, never to rise again. It will be conquered by each of us taking responsibility for its existence in any area of human activity and endeavor that we control or influence. We will overcome as we are honest enough with our own faults to ask for forgiveness and to make right, as far as possible, what we have done wrong. We will overcome as we appeal to God to move the stones of evil out of our lives and rest in the assurance that He will. We will overcome as we accept and forgive those who ask our forgiveness for who they have become instead of who they were when they injured us. We will overcome as we become active in leading victims of evil to the shelter of heaven and helping them to recover. We will overcome as we demonstrate courage, decency, and nobility of character in all circumstances of life. We will overcome as we fully commit to aligning ourselves with God and opposing evil wherever we find it with patience, perseverance, consistency, and determination. We will overcome when we refuse to ever fight evil with evil, for heaven is persistent, benevolent, consistent opposition to everything that is evil.

It is not enough to fight evil and create a vacuum.[61] We need the help of the same Divine Invisible Being to fill life with all that is not evil; we need to give heaven to others.

Chapter 5
GIVING *IS* HEAVEN

Steven Armstrong walked into his third grade classroom with a big question. What was all the excitement on this Friday morning? Why was Martin Luther King Jr. dead?

Steven's teacher had a big answer. Jane Elliott knew her Iowan students didn't understand racial injustice. They had never seen people of a different skin color. They had never experienced how unfairly black people were treated in other places. Ms. Elliot asked her students if they wanted to know what it felt like to receive discrimination. They said, "Yes."

So on that Friday, Ms. Elliot separated her students by eye color. Her brown and green-eyed students were the first[62] to be superior, noted as being "cleaner" and "smarter." They got to go back through line for a second time at lunch. They got an extra five minutes at recess. They could play on the new jungle gym.

All her blue-eyed students had to wear a green armband made of construction paper. The blue-eyed children had to use paper cups at the water fountain that the brown-eyed students were free to use. They didn't get to go back through the line for a second time at lunch. They didn't get an extra five minutes at recess. They couldn't play on the new jungle gym.

All of these commands were given abruptly along with statements saying that brown-eyed students were smarter. Little mistakes of blue-eyed students were magnified to prove that they were in fact less intelligent and less desirable.

By afternoon, several of Jane's brown-eyed students were doing better on their tests and confidently took leadership roles. Her blue-eyed students became timid followers, and even those who never made mistakes struggled with getting the correct answers while doing their school work. A fight broke out, started by some of those who resented being reminded that they were "blue-eyed." During recess time, some brown-eyed girls banded together and made a normally bright blue-eyed girl apologize to them for acting like she was superior to her brown-eyed colleagues.

Monday morning, Jane switched her students' roles, explaining that she had made a mistake the previous school day. She rewarded blue-eyed students with the privileges of going through the line for a second time at lunch, having an extra five minutes at recess, and accessing the new jungle gym.

Ms. Elliot publicly humiliated her brown-eyed students as inferior and not smart. Monday afternoon she stopped the experiment, asking her students to write about their experience. When this lesson on racism ended, the all-white class had a first-hand glimpse into the reason that Martin Luther King, Jr. lost his life to an assassin's bullet. Decades later, they still remember the lesson.

That was April of 1968. Ms. Elliot has continued demonstrating the same lesson for more than four decades. Even after she left the teaching profession, she continued to guide the exercise on eye color for various government, military, and corporate groups. [63] It is a simple exercise that teaches us a basic fact: many of us treat people who are different than we are unfairly.

Recognizing that we treat different people differently is difficult. Recognizing that other people treat us differently is easy to do. Sometimes the easiest way to recognize our own behavior is to spend a little time living with those who are different than we are and experience life as they do.

In November and December of 1959, John Griffin traveled through Louisiana, Mississippi, Alabama, and Georgia. As a Caucasian with artificially darkened skin, he experienced life as unfairly as African-Americans did. In his memoir, *Black Like Me,* he wrote of having trouble finding basic things like food and a bathroom. He told of being lonely, feeling hopeless, experiencing hatred, and being treated unfairly just because people thought he was black. He came to appreciate the experiences, the kindnesses, and injustices that African-Americans around him were going through by living among them, as one of them. His book was frank and insightful. It exposed many white-skinned people to a view of what some of them were doing. Before his writing about the events he endured was published, word escaped about his experiment and he was regarded no differently than when his skin was dark, even to the point of being sought out by the Ku Klux Klan. A short time later, he and his family left the United States for Mexico to live awhile there in exile. *Smithsonian Magazine* noted of Griffin's work, "John Howard Griffin changed more than the color of his skin. He helped change the way America saw itself."[64] His work contributed to a shift in behavior by many southern Caucasians.

Nothing will ever justify the injuries experienced by American slaves and their descendants. Nothing can. Although not as extreme, other injustices have found many victims, and they do not restrict themselves to one's skin color. In truth, we could write many books to expose discrimination: *One-legged Like Me, Ugly Like Me, Illiterate Like Me, Poor Like Me, Overweight Like Me.* Each book would reveal the sad story of the injustices that so many have received for qualities they could not change at the time.

Sometimes it seems as if our world has forgotten that behind every label is a person. Short or tall, black or white, blue-eyed or brown-eyed, timid or courageous: none of these "labels" changes the humanity of a person. Conservatives have red blood flowing in their arteries just as certainly as do liberals. Those who don't attend church have emotions that need consideration in exactly the same way as those who do attend church. The Palestinian has a mind and a heart as much as the Israeli. The Lutheran, the Mormon, the Sikh, the Falun Gong, the Methodist, the Baha'i, the Baptist, the Pentecostal, and the pagan all share the human need to be loved and respected.

Many American people have made the fair treatment of certain races and ethnicities an important issue. This is good, but it does not go far enough. Every injustice against another human is the rejection of heaven and the promotion of hell. We should never stop until each human stands integrated into a community that values, respects, and honors one another. In the words of Dr. King's famous "I Have a Dream" speech, "Now is the time to make justice a reality for all of God's children."[65]

The Solution to Injustice

Jesus discussed social justice in Matthew 5:43–48.

> "Ye have heard that it hath been said, Thou shalt love thy neighbour, and hate thine enemy. But I say unto you, Love your enemies, bless them that curse you, do good to them that hate you, and pray for them which despitefully use you, and persecute you; that ye may be the children of your Father which is in heaven: for he maketh his sun to rise on the evil and on the good, and sendeth rain on the just and on the unjust. For if ye love them which love you, what reward have ye? do not even

the publicans the same? And if ye salute your brethren only, what do ye more than others? do not even the publicans so? Be ye therefore perfect, even as your Father which is in heaven is perfect."

The greatest solution to all social harm is the individual commitment first to "love the Lord your God with all your heart, with all your soul, and with all your mind … [and second] love your neighbor as yourself" (Matthew 22:37, 39). You don't need any religion to love other brown-eyed people better that blue-eyed people. You don't need any philosophy to love other blue-eyed people better than brown-eyed people. Instead, it takes heaven to completely overcome *all* prejudice. It takes heaven to treat every human fairly, firmly, and kindly.

God has no prejudice. He doesn't send rain to only brown-eyed people. He doesn't send sunshine to only blue-eyed people. He doesn't love only "good" people. He doesn't help only His favorites. He never discriminates. We become mature (perfect), like God is mature, when we do not ever treat another human being unjustly.

Also, God has no discrimination in spiritual matters like salvation and power and wisdom, either. He saves the worst and the best. He uses the worst and the best. Murderers have been some of God's most useful and effective servants. Think of Moses, David, and Paul. The first two committed murder; the last one assisted in genocide, yet God forgave and used all of them for causes greater than they could ever have imagined. Together they wrote more than one third of the text of the Bible. History demonstrates that no one is too evil for the grace of God.

We have drawn too narrow a definition of discrimination. It is no disrespect to those who have suffered for the color of their skin to acknowledge that discrimination includes any act of injustice to another human being. [66] We have argued for too little in discussing social justice. Let us never settle, let us never stop so long as one of God's children is treated unjustly and we can do anything about it. After all, heaven is not about treating people the way they *deserve* to be treated. It is about treating them the way they were *created* to be treated. Every action toward another human must be a reflection of the value God has given to that person. We must treat them as a child of the Divine and not according to who they "are" or what they have done.

We need to distinguish between people and actions. Actions are right or wrong. Actions are good or bad. People are important

Everyone is valuable. I may enjoy or dislike the actions of my friends and family, but I regard and respect every human being.

In society, we may identify and even punish certain actions. Actions that harm others are destructive to society. Murder, rape, stealing, lying, and betraying promises all destroy our society. But the people who committed these horrible actions are still important. God values every person without respect to their behavior. When we accept heaven, we will mimic God and do the same.

We should never speak derogatorily about anyone. We should never speak nastily toward anyone. No matter their politics or actions, no matter their ideas or how they look, we never have an excuse to hurt a fellow human being unnecessarily. Even if someone hurts us, we still do not have permission to treat them like less than the valuable person they are or to wrong them in return. *Two wrong actions don't make a right one.* We should never see others as more or less valuable than us. So long as we all depend on the same red blood and oxygen for life, we are equally important and valuable. The famed Golden Rule is the ultimate weapon against all injustice. Act toward everyone else by the standard of behavior that you would like to be used toward you (see Matthew 7:12).

This is not to suggest that all humans can do the same work or that they will reach all the same intellectual conclusions. Heaven does not destroy individuality nor order nor authority nor make every person the cookie-cutter image of everyone else. This is not to suggest that we should ever ignore accountability. On the contrary, Heaven looks out for the well-being of and acknowledges the individuality, the needs, and the concerns of every person on the planet.

Heaven is a new social order. We are used to maintaining friendships that get by, that make us feel comfortable. That will not work eternally. Heaven means eventually being friends with every human and being friends forever. That starts now. It means having friendships that are fair and nurturing, always. [67]

Heaven also means serving each person as they come into our lives, according to the abilities and resources we have been given (see 1 Corinthians 12:1–11). In the words of George Bernard Shaw, "I am of the opinion that my life belongs to the whole community, and as long as I live, it is my privilege to do for it whatever I can." [68] The apostle Paul spoke of serving others as a debt we owe society. [69] We are here to give to our fellow humans. Everyone can give simple attention, a smile, or a handshake, for each of us has different abilities and strengths that we can use to benefit others. [70]

Let us treat both those who are kind to us and those who hurt us with dignity, thoughtfulness, generosity, equality, and justice.

Many times, however, we don't want to give heaven to others. Sometimes this is because we are afraid that the other person will hurt us; thus, we entrench ourselves in self-pity and hang on to the memories of others hurting us. We are determined to make sure that the other person receives all the hell we can send their way. Nonetheless, giving hell *is* hell, and therefore never really satisfying. It may feel good to hurt someone at first, but it won't feel good forever.

At other times, we are just lazy. We don't care. We simply want to be treated wonderfully, and we have no problem with hurting others in the process. That is selfish and destructive. As we hurt others, they want to hurt us and still others; these actions become a vicious cycle, resulting in a steady stream of pain and injury that becomes an ocean of sorrow and hostility.

Heaven is interested in the eternal happiness of every person we interact with. Heaven appreciates the virtues of each one of us. Heaven understands the weaknesses and faults of each of us and never exploits that knowledge. Heaven is honest without being cruel. Heaven gives goodwill to all who will accept it, and is kind in its firmness with those who reject goodwill. There is so much that we can do for others. There is so much we can give to them. [71]

Manifesting heaven to others is a choice to be understanding and sympathetic. It is a choice to hold others accountable and to be grateful when others hold us accountable. It is the determination to be responsible and loving and giving in our social relationships. It is our desire to share our joy in life rather than spread pain. It is the commitment to be honest about what hurts us without trying to binge on pity. It is the dedication to nurture and protect individuality without making individuality our god. It is the commitment to encourage natural diversity without allowing that diversity to anger us or to become our obsession. It is the choice to accept different viewpoints and ideas while holding people accountable for ideas and actions that hurt us or others.

We could call it love. We could say that heaven is loving every person you ever meet or influence, but that word "love" is so bent and twisted and abused that it might be misunderstood.

Giving heaven to others takes courage. It is risky. It can leave us vulnerable, but it beats all the other alternatives the world can offer. The rewards may not all come at once, but they are certain. Love will triumph. Even if it suffers along the way, it will ultimately win.

Victory over evil only comes from heaven. Heaven is a four-part harmony between who you are, what you get, what you refuse, and what you give. It is choosing the best attitude in every moment, making the best of every circumstance. It is reaching out and accepting God and depending on Him. It is persistent, benevolent, consistent opposition to everything that is evil. It is giving to others the kind of relationship we want to receive.

Nevertheless, this four-part harmony may still be confusing to some of us. We may still uncertain about it, so let's take a look at what causes our confusion.

Clearing up Confusion

Over the last four chapters, we looked at heaven. We challenged ourselves to define it and determined how to reach it. We looked at its costs and benefits and challenges. Still, this is not enough.

Our world has asserted that feeling good is the only heaven that any of us need. We are encouraged to find whatever makes us happy and do it with abandon. This book has already stated that doing what we hope will make us feel good is not the same as heaven and that heaven is richer and grander than merely feeling good for the moment. It has already been pointed out that the sacrifice and discipline involved in experiencing heaven are worth the richer reward that they bring.

Unfortunately, in our world, we find these arguments confusing sometimes. People try to convince us that the heaven presented here simply doesn't work. Two arguments are commonly raised against the heaven offered in these pages:

1. Heaven won't let you be happy or have fun at all.

2. Heaven doesn't exist because evil does.

The next two chapters will examine these objections in detail, offering what are believed to be compelling reasons why they are excuses and distractions. You will be the judge of whether or not this is correct.

Chapter 6
PLEASURE SHOULD NEVER INJURE

Albert Gregory was one of those dashing young Englishmen in the nineteenth century on a job hunt. He travelled by train to a city near London called Harrow. Greg, as we'll nickname him, was as smart as he was good-looking. He used his intelligence to gather the best recommendations his town could provide. The preacher and several local businessmen provided letters of recommendation or "testimonials" of Greg's fine ability and affability.

Greg was charming, but when he was bored he usually got himself into trouble. After riding a few miles on the train, the excitement of the trip began to wear off. When he became disinterested, Greg figured out just what he could do next.

Perhaps the idea came to him when he was watching passengers as they boarded the train at the station. An old farmer climbed on and looked bewildered. He stumbled into a seat in front of Greg. His weathered face looked worried, like he was searching for someone to help. This may have been the old man's first trip on anything faster than a horse. Soon the conductor came by, and the farmer stopped him with a timid question.

"When do we get to Harrow?"

"Eight-thirty this evening" was the busy reply as the conductor moved on.

The old man muttered under his breath to no one in particular, "After dark, after dark! And there's no moon. I won't know where to go!"

Just then the conductor returned, and the old man asked a favor.

"Mr. Conductor, how will I know when to get out? I've never been to Harrow. I don't want to get out at the wrong place."

The face and the body pleaded more than words could ever do. The poor man seemed alone, helpless, and lost.

The conductor assured him, "Don't worry. I will tell you when we reach Harrow. I won't forget you."

This seemed to soothe the old man's mind, and he sat back and soon fell asleep.

Albert watched the man sleeping on the bench in front of him. The wheels turned thousands of times, taking them toward London. Day turned to night. Those gas lights used in railroad cars before electricity were lit. The train was still a few miles away when it came to a stop in a small village. At that very stop, Greg decided play the joke he had been planning all afternoon.

He jumped up and leaned over the white hairs in front of him. Shaking the sleeping passenger violently, he told him to get off quick. This was Harrow station, and the train was about to leave with him still on the train.

The old farmer was startled. He wasn't used to trains and didn't know where he was. He knew that this boy wasn't the conductor but figured it was someone the conductor had sent, so he got off.

"Can you tell me where I might find the lawyer Harrington?" the farmer asked the station manager.

"Never heard that name."

"Isn't this Harrow?"

"No. This is Whipple."

"I got off at the wrong station! What can I do now?"

"Stay at the motel next to the train station."

There was nothing else he could do.

But sleep didn't come easily for him in that strange place. The boy had tricked him, so he had to spend money the farm had not yet earned.

The next morning, the farmer was at the train station early. Earnestly, he waited for the train. Finally, the whistle blew, and the steam engine chugged to a stop.

A plain-looking boy stepped up to the old man and asked, "Can I help you board the train?"

Young Lyman Dean took the old, worn arm and gently steadied the farmer's steps. Together they found a seat. "Thank you, my boy. I am getting old and clumsy. A little help from a young hand comes timely. Where are you going?"

"To Harrow. I saw a job advertised to work as a salesman in a store there. I am going to apply for it."

"I hope you get it. You have been a good help to me. I am sure you will be a good help there too. I am also going to Harrow. I need to visit the attorney Aaron Harrington, but I've had problems getting to his office.

"On the way to the train station, the stage coach broke down, and I missed the train. Then some boy tricked me and told me to get out at the wrong station. I hope I don't have any more problems."

"I am sorry you've had such a difficult trip. But don't worry. I've been to Harrow many times. I know just where Mr. Harrington's office is located. I will be happy to help you to get off at the right station and reach his office."

"Thank you."

"The pleasure is mine," Lyman said with a smile. He meant it too.

Half an hour later, Lyman helped the old farmer off the train and walked with him to the office of Aaron Harrington, Esquire.

"Thank you, Lyman. And one more favor. Could you tell me where to find Luke Conway's Store?"

"That's just the store I am going to right now for work. It's around the corner and down two blocks."

"Lyman, you've really been a big help to me. I wish I could do something for you in return. Luke Conway knows me. I am coming to see him next. If you apply for the job before I get there, tell him that Gideon Randal is your friend. Good-bye."

The attorney wasn't in the office. Fifteen minutes later, Gideon opened the door to Mr. Conway's office.

"Do you remember me, Luke?"

"Gideon! Remember you? I can't ever forget you! How could I? I was cold and hungry. You found me. I was forgotten and without a friend in the whole world. You took me in. Thirty years ago you fed me; you gave me work; you treated me like your own son. Your wife sewed clothes for me with her own hands. You paid for me to start my first business. I would still be helpless and hopeless if you hadn't cared for me, loved me, believed in me. This store is because of you! Gideon, my success is because of you! Repay you, I *cannot*. Forget you, I *will* not!"

"How is MarthaAnn? How is the farm? How are you?"

"Not so well, Luke. The farm hasn't been producing well in the last few years. I needed money to survive, and I had to borrow. I borrowed from Eugene Harrington. I put my house up as collateral for the loan. When Eugene died unexpectedly, his son Aaron tried to foreclose on me and take the house. I tried to come and talk to Mr. Harrington, but I had two accidents on the way. The carriage broke down on the way to the train station and delayed me half a day. Then a boy tricked me and told me to get out at Whipple Village last night.

"Finally, this morning I came to try to talk to Harrington, but he was out of the office."

"Oh, I *can* repay you a little! I will pay the mortgage. Don't worry about the debt and your farm. I can easily afford to cover that. Just let me hire one of these two boys here as a salesman for my store, and then I will take you to my home."

Turning to the boys he said, "I suppose you came to apply for the job I advertised."

"Yes," came the response.

"You came first. What is your name?"

"I'm Albert Gregory. I can suit you well. I have reference letters from the local pastor and from businessmen from my town recommending me."

"I don't need your letters. I think I know more about you than you expect. You didn't know it, but last night I boarded the train in the town of Whipple to come to Harrow. In the seat behind me was a boy bragging about how he intended to come to my store this morning and apply for the job I am offering. He talked about having letters from the very people you just mentioned. Then he proceeded to talk a lot more about his 'fun.'

"Apparently, he tricked an old man into getting out at Whipple by telling him that the stop was Harrow. I heard that young man laugh and laugh at how foolish the old man was to get out of the train. I heard 'Ha, ha! I did think the old fool would hear the station called. I didn't think he would leave the train.' A little later I heard, 'I didn't think he would get past the door! To think he went out on the platform and got left behind! What a delicious old simpleton! What a naive fool! He BELIEVED me when I said Harrow. Ha, ha.'"

"Gideon, do you recognize this boy?"

The farmer looked intently at him for a moment.

"Why it is. He is the boy who tricked me last night. I am sure it is."

"Mr. Gregory, you will not make a good salesman in my store. You are not happy helping customers, or strangers, or old men riding trains. You are happy laughing at them and tricking them. You get your joy from other people's pain. I cannot hire you. Your references only hide the facts of who you really are."

Turning to the other boy he asked, "What is your name?"

"Lyman Dean. I would be happy to work hard for you. My mother is poor. I want to earn my living. But I don't have any reference letters for you."

"Oh yes you do," said the farmer, who was looking for a chance to say something.

"Luke, this boy helped me get on the train this morning. He helped me find a seat and get off at the right station. He walked with me to

Harrington's office and told me where to find you. He did it all with a smile and as though he enjoyed it. I am sure he can help you, your customers, and even old men like me."

"Lyman, if you find happiness in helping others, I believe you will be happy to help my customers. You can begin right now. I am happy to hire you."[72]

Sitting in that store business office were two contrasting examples of pleasure. Greg seemed happiest when he was *hurting* others. Lyman was happiest in *helping* others. Thus, into these very simplistic categories, *helpful* or *harmful*, all of pleasure fits.

Is Pleasure Good?

The subject of pleasure is important in understanding heaven because the pursuit of pleasure is one of the most common arguments used against it. It is suggested that developing healthy attitudes, trusting in an unseen God, battling against corruption, and being socially fair is hard work and prevents one from being truly happy. Supposedly, happiness is found in pursuing pleasure without regard to personal character or social harm. Let us open-mindedly consider the value and the danger in pleasure.

Let us start with the question: should we have pleasure? Throughout recorded history some have taken satisfaction in teaching that pleasure is dangerous. They seem to believe that happy people are evil people. They promote ideas that we should reject anything that has pleasure; instead, we should glory in pain for the sake of pain.

Can we have pleasure and be decent and reasonable people at the same time? This more fundamental question ought to have an extremely obvious answer, but the idea that we ought to be afraid of and even resent pleasure is so widespread that it must be addressed. Its pernicious shadow has darkened our concepts of recreation, marriage, work, and socializing. This falsehood has lured many people into promoting evil by claiming that we must choose between mild forms of evil or having no pleasure at all. An obvious example is the assertion that we can only choose between sexual promiscuity and being miserable prudes. Therefore, it is suggested that those who demonstrate commitment and loyalty to one spouse must be doing it because they are dedicated to living without pleasure! Those who use this argument seem to almost deny that a couple can live together decade after decade and be happy.

Is it reasonable to be happy? God is happy. He talks about His pleasures and tells us what makes Him happy and what doesn't.

- *God enjoys what He accomplishes*: "The Lord shall rejoice in his works" (Psalm 104:31).

- *God enjoys people*: "I will ... joy in my people" (Isaiah 65:19).

- *God enjoys humans so much that He sings about them*: "The Lord thy God in the midst of thee is mighty; He will save, he will rejoice over thee with joy; he will rest in his love, he will joy over thee with singing" (Zephaniah 3:17).

- *God enjoys our prosperity*: "Let the Lord be magnified, which hath pleasure in the prosperity of his servant" (Psalm 35:27).

- *God doesn't enjoy death; not even the death of those who hate and hurt Him*: "Have I any pleasure at all that the wicked should die? saith the Lord God: and not that he should return from his ways, and live? ... I have no pleasure in the death of him that dieth, saith the Lord God: wherefore turn yourselves, and live ye" (Ezekiel 18:23, 32).

God is a joyful being. He enjoys life. He enjoys friends. He doesn't enjoy injury or death. It is true that He allows things that He doesn't enjoy and gives life to those who hurt Him, but He is a happy Being who experiences lots of pleasure.

God made us in His image (see Genesis 1:26). He designed us to be happy and to enjoy life.

"No man can find out the work that God maketh from the beginning to the end. I know that there is no good in them, but for a man to rejoice, and to do good in his life.... every man should eat and drink, and enjoy the good of all his labour, it is the gift of God" (Ecclesiastes 3:11–13).

"The poor among men shall rejoice in the Holy One of Israel" (Isaiah 29:19).

"Let the heart of them rejoice that seek the Lord" (Psalm 105:3).

"The ransomed of the Lord ... shall come to Zion with songs and everlasting joy upon their heads: they shall obtain joy and gladness, and sorrow and sighing shall flee away" (Isaiah 35:10).

"Our heart shall rejoice in him, because we have trusted in his holy name" (Psalm 33:21).

"They shall be abundantly satisfied with the fatness of thy house; and thou shalt make them drink of the river of thy pleasures" (Psalm 36:8).

"Restore unto me the joy of thy salvation; and uphold me with thy free spirit" (Psalm 51:12).

"Thou wilt shew me the path of life: in thy presence is fulness of joy; at thy right hand there are pleasures for evermore" (Psalm 16:11).

The Bible plainly teaches us that a joyful Divinity designed for us to be a joyful humanity.

Hellish Pleasure versus Heavenly Pleasure

Still, not all pleasure is joyful. As the story of Greg and his trick on the farmer who boarded the train pointed out, what might be pleasure for one can be hurtful and sometimes downright destructive for another. This illustrates why we need to expand our moral definitions of crime. [73]

For example, God broadens the definition of murder to include hatred and resentment. "Whoever hates his brother man is a murderer" (1 John 3:15 NKJV, also noted in Matthew 5:21–24).

Let's move past our simplistic ideas about murder and suicide. Bitterness toward your spouse or family member is a subtle form of killing them. Intentionally ignoring someone as a form of cruelty is a subtle way to "help" them toward death. Taunting, intimidating, and belittling another shortens the quality and sometimes the quantity of that person's life. These evil behaviors are a subtle form of murder. Anyone who enjoys causing others pain may be seeking their own pleasure, but they are promoting hell for the receiving party. Their actions are a direct contribution to the sum total of evil in our world.

Let's expand our understanding of murder to include those actions, no matter how large or small, that directly or indirectly injure others. Let's also expand our understanding of suicide to include those actions, no matter how large or small, that directly or indirectly injure oneself. If I smoke cigarettes, and those cigarettes cause me to die five years sooner than I otherwise would have, every inhalation of smoke that I took was an act of suicide. If the same smoke causes someone else to die prematurely, I am a murderer as well. Both are morally criminal, no matter how enjoyable they seem to me as I do them.

The popular moral argument to do whatever feels good is one of the greatest sources of evil in our world today. It is used over and over to justify harming ourselves and each other. It is false. Equally false is the popular moral argument that we cannot be happy when we exercise personal discipline and manifest personal integrity. Doing good and being happy are not mutually exclusive.

Let's stop arguing in favor of the flavor of food at any cost to our health. Let stop arguing for sexual pleasure at any cost to our families, communities, and world. Let's stop arguing in favor of the promotion of fantasy stories at any cost to the education of ethics and morality to ourselves, our children, and our world. Let's stop arguing in favor of going to any extreme to make our bodies appear "beautiful" at any cost to our health, self-esteem, and well-being. Let's stop with any pleasure that destroys us as humans.

It is time to acknowledge that we can have rich flavor and health. We can have sexual contentment and a strong family. We can have entertaining stories that reinforce good ethics. We can look good, and have health and self-esteem. We can ride the train without tricking the old man in front of us. It just takes a little more self-control, a little more hard work, and a little more determination than the Greg in us wants. It may well take more than we have, until we ask God to remove the stones out of our way.

Governing our wants and desires while striving for excellence is not a return to living in a cave. It is the path to being truly civilized. It is a return of the human race to the God-likeness from which we have fallen.

As humans, we have focused on a few pleasures that contain very destructive elements, such as smoking. Our world, nevertheless, is filled with pleasures made by God Himself, and we humans have barely discovered the "tip of the iceberg." We have no idea what future joys are awaiting us.

I love the look in a young student's eyes when he or she understands a new math concept and how it works in his or her everyday life. I love reaching the pinnacle of a life mountain and looking down on my own history. I love drinking in the colors of the sunrise and the sunset. I love the flavors of tropical fruit. I love the smell of fresh, homemade bread. I love the touch of smooth surfaces. I love discovering new geographical locations. I love successfully negotiating a business deal.

love talking with my friends. I love discovering spiritual truths and how they coincide with social and physical reality. I love the acceptance and appreciation provided to me by my family and friends. I love intimacy with great thoughts, with my environment, with my family, with my community, and with God.

In those moments when God seems to speak out of the silence, my thoughts race in ways I could never anticipate or conceive of. I lose all sense of anything else but my thoughts. My emotions are excited by the simple compelling message of those thoughts. Listening to God is the highest pleasure, the strongest emotional and physical experience I've ever discovered. The prophet Daniel says his reaction to hearing God's voice was so strong that he fell as one dead. [74]

This list is only the beginning. You will be able to compose your own list drawn from the thousands of pleasures from your own experiences. Isaac Newton is quoted as acknowledging the vastness of our world that is yet to be discovered. "I don't know what I may appear to the world, but to myself, I seem to have been only like a boy playing on the sea-shore and diverting myself in now and then finding a smoother pebble or a prettier shell than ordinary, whilst the great ocean of truth lay all undiscovered before me." [75]

If we do not see the vast expanse of pleasure waiting for us, then maybe it is because we are not used to seeing what is right in front of us. Apparently, a young man learned this in a strange way. He wanted to study from one of Europe's most prestigious medical doctors a few centuries ago. (This was back when medicine was studied by apprenticeship rather than at medical school.) The doctor who was his counselor seemed too busy for the ambitious student. He took the young man, sat him in front of a fish, and asked the student to make a drawing of the fish. It didn't take him long to sketch the animal. When the student showed the picture to his new mentor, the doctor sent him back to draw a better copy.

The doctor left the student in front of the fish all day, which frustrated the ambitious young man. The student returned the next day, only to be given the same task. This frustrated him even more. As a result, he thought of quitting. However, he knew of no other opportunity in all of Europe as good as this one to learn medicine, so he sat there and stared at the fish a second day.

On the third day, the physician sent him back to the same fish. He sat in boredom and frustration again. Only then did he begin to see the details: the details of the individual scales, the patterns, and the tiniest intricacies. His pen started to move rapidly. He became engrossed with the fish. He was so busy that he didn't even notice the famed doctor, but the doctor noticed him. Interrupting the student from his lesson on the fish, the doctor smiled and said, "Now you are ready to learn! Come with me."

How many times do we see the fish and still not see the fish? How many times do we have eyes and still not see? How many times do we miss the joy and pleasure in front of us because a little bit of time and work are involved?

In a world filled with more beneficial pleasure than we have discovered or can even imagine, do we still need anything harmful? Can we tolerate a little bit of evil, especially if it is convenient? Is mild destruction acceptable in pursuit of enjoyment?

A previous chapter about the war against evil, "A Heavenly Battle," should have already answered these questions. For those who still want to hang on to a bit of doubt, here is a little more to consider.

- David spoke of Jesus as One who "love[s] the right and hate[s] the wrong" (Psalm 45:7 *The Message*).

- John told us that Jesus will exclude everything that is shameful, impure, or dishonest from the universe (Revelation 21:27, paraphrased).

- Isaiah observed a time when "they shall not hurt nor destroy in all my holy mountain: for the earth shall be full of the knowledge of the Lord" (Isaiah 11:9).

These few verses, and the many more that corroborate them, clearly state that one day we will be free of any evil pleasure, no matter how harmless it may seem. Heaven simply has no room or necessity for anything remotely destructive.

We need to be *in control* of our desires rather than *being controlled* by them. If a desire injures us, others, our environment, or God Himself, we need to give it up, throw it out, and reject it. If it is a pleasure that harms, run away from it. Refuse. Find something else. Just never do it. *Never.*

What can we do if we have made a religion out of feeling good? What if gratification is the only god we worship? If we are really to monitor and discipline our actions so that they contribute to innocent pleasure and never to destruction, *how do we do it*? How can we accomplish such a level of personal control over our own desires and actions?

Prayer is the tool that God gave us to change ourselves. Prayer is not about changing God's mind, but about changing our hearts. "Your Father knows what you need before you ask him" (Matthew 6:8 RSV). Prayer does not bring God down to us, but it lifts us up to Him. It is His way of changing us so that we are ready to receive Him. It is where we ask for His help removing the rocks that litter our lives. It is where we recognize the little evils that contaminate us and get in the way of heaven. In the quiet, let us ask God to identify His desire for us and make plain what we can do to cooperate. Whatever thoughts and plans He gives us, let us appreciate, not repudiate. He will change our desires and give us the power to do well, always.

> "Let not sin therefore reign in your mortal body, that ye should obey it in the lusts thereof. Neither yield ye your members as instruments of unrighteousness unto sin: but yield yourselves unto God ... For sin shall not have dominion over you" (Romans 6:12–14).

> "Denying ungodliness and worldly lusts, we should live soberly, righteously, and godly, in this present world; looking for ... the glorious appearing of ... our Saviour Jesus Christ; who gave himself for us, that he might redeem us from all iniquity, and purify unto himself a peculiar people, zealous of good works" (Titus 2:12–14).

There is no room for the argument that heaven and happiness can't get along. We do not have to do a certain amount of evil (we are always told that it is mild evil) to be content. We can be joyful because God is a joyful Being. He is personally committed to our contentment, our joy. Anytime we ask, He will change us into people committed to successfully appreciating the innocent pleasures heaven gives us. With His support, we can live happy, evil-free lives. There is no justification for the argument repeated relentlessly in a variety of forms that we need to keep evil around just to be happy.

Chapter 7
PAIN IS NEVER IN VAIN

Many of us find pain and sorrow difficult to accept or appreciate. We resist any explanation that would justify their existence. Sorrow is an ugly thing. It is unnatural. Many believe it is impossible to understand. Certainly it is difficult to explain when you experience it. We do not like pain. Instead of embracing it, we look for ways to avoid heartache. We work hard to banish all anguish. Nevertheless, it is still here with us.

The Language of Pain

Pain is a language all its own. It communicates to all of us that something is wrong. In a simple form, pain tells us to stop and change what we are doing. When you spend too long hunched over your computer or your garden, your back says, "Ouch!" Pain tells you to straighten your back. When you warm your hands near a fire on a cold day and they begin to hurt, you know to move away from the fire.

Without pain, our lives would be terrible. Just ask people with leprosy. This disease damages nerves until no pain is felt by the sufferer. When people with leprosy get burned, they do not feel the pain. They don't have any sensation that tells them to move away from the fire or stove. They don't react to mosquitoes and bigger animals biting them. Nothing tells their body to change, so they damage or lose body parts without realizing what they are doing. Life without pain is terrible. [76]

Life with pain is also difficult. This is true wherever that pain comes from. We hurt ourselves. As children, we stumble and fall and get hurt. As young people, we often make little choices that come back to haunt us with big consequences. As adults, we make choices that haunt our families and friends with even bigger consequences. Whether we fall off a motorcycle and break our ribs or trust someone without considering how likely they are to betray us, we know and understand the pain that we cause ourselves.

It's the pain others cause us that angers us more. When I stretch my legs out in front of where someone is running and he or she falls and sprains an ankle, that ankle hurts to tell that individual that something is wrong inside his or her body. That person's mind also tells him or her that I was wrong to stretch out my legs in the path so he or she would trip. The pain of that individual is communicated to both of us. The pain experienced is also insulting. Any pain that is caused by someone else angers us. Naturally, we tend to want revenge. It is one thing to cry with pain from a sprained ankle. It is another to actually kill for being tripped up.

When parents divorce, their children experience pain that has nothing to do with that child's own mistakes. Children do not cause the experience of abandonment that haunts many of them because of their parents' divorce. Nevertheless, they feel the pain, which was caused by their parents. Many children of divorce believe they are responsible for their parents having grown apart and/or becoming bitter.[77] Pain tells these children that somehow those parents could not find the commitment or the social tools to happily trust each other and keep a working relationship that nurtured their children.

We are often hurt by other people. We have to find tools and methods to handle that pain. We also have to find the social tools to communicate to others that they are injuring us without allowing ourselves to injure them. It is one thing to be hurt by the parents' divorce. It is another thing to behave as nastily as possible while around either of your parents just to hurt one or the other back. We have to stand up for ourselves while standing apart from the culture of unnecessarily injuring others. Many adults struggle with being able to acquire this trait, much less children.[78]

This world is filled with pain that comes from others. War is a prominent example. Consider, for instance, the Rwandan lady in chapter 4 that was injured by her own neighbor.

Then there is the pain that angers us most. It is the pain that seems unprovoked: childhood leukemia, victims of lightning strikes, children born without limbs. This pain seems so senseless and unexplainable. Philosophers have tried for centuries to explain it. Few have given any satisfying answers. We see the pain. Maybe we experience it. We are helpless in the face of it. Why?

The best explanation for apparently senseless suffering comes from understanding yet another kind of pain.

The ultimate experience in pain is observed in personal sacrifice. This is pain that is chosen. We volunteer for it. Firefighters enter a burning building knowing that they may suffer for the rest of their lives from what they are doing. They still choose to go in (when they can choose not to), but going in is a sacrifice for a greater good. They risk their comfort, and possibly even lives, to save other lives. The lives of the people inside the burning building mean more to the firefighters than their own comfort.

The heroism of those who go out of their way during wartime to protect their comrades and innocent bystanders illustrates this kind of pain. When a soldier falls on a mortar, knowing it will injure or kill him, just to save the others around him, we see this ultimate sacrifice. We see it also in the martyrs to the development of human scientific knowledge. Marie Curie, who sacrificed her life in the pursuit of scientific knowledge,[79] chose that kind of noble suffering that contributes to our overall accumulation of knowledge.

The life of nuclear scientist Louis Slotin is another example. Slotin sacrificed his own life for the benefit of our knowledge of nuclear reaction, dying as a hero to many.

After World War II, the Hungarian-Canadian scientist grew weary of participating in nuclear research for the purpose of creating bombs.[80] In training his replacement, he demonstrated for Alvin C. Graves and six others how to generate a plutonium bomb by bringing it to a critical state. On May 21, 1946, while Slotin was holding the one half sphere of plutonium over the bottom half sphere, the screwdriver that separated the two pieces of plutonium slipped out of his hand and created a supercritical situation by allowing the two hemispheres to meet.

Slotin pulled the pieces apart quickly, bringing the chain reaction to a halt. The men dashed from the laboratory, called the authorities, and sat outside that afternoon as calmly as possible. They then documented where each person stood in the room. Slotin died nine days later from the radiation poisoning.[81]

The diagram that recorded where each person was located at the moment of the accident provided some of the earliest information on how close to radiation someone needed to be for radiation injury to occur and to what extent the injury would occur. Slotin's increased exposure and consequent death provided science with information that could not otherwise have been gathered. He was a martyr on behalf of science. This concept of martyrdom for the sake of knowledge brings us back to the previous kind of pain, apparently senseless pain.

Pain—the Price of Moral Knowledge

We sometimes forget how much our knowledge today costs. In our Western culture where knowledge is celebrated, it is easy to explore and attain more knowledge. This is not, however, the case everywhere or all the time. One of the most costly gains in knowledge by humanity has been the knowledge of the value of freedom and how to get and keep it.

Freedom is not only the opportunity to do what you think is right, but it is also the opportunity to do what everyone else thinks is wrong. Freedom, particularly the opportunity to do what everyone else thinks is wrong, is hard for us as humans to give to each other. Millions of people throughout history have lived under the tyrannical control of other humans who attempted to control their behavior. Freedom is something that has been experienced only by a minority of the human population. Our freedom today to do what others think is wrong is directly traceable to the deaths of thousands of people in the 1500s, including some Italians.

For several centuries before the 1500s, the Waldensian population of several thousand people lived in the Alps of northern Italy. South and east of them in the valleys was a much larger population. Often tension arose between this mountain people and their neighbors in the plain, even though generally there was some level of toleration between the peoples. [82]

After the Protestant Reformation occurred in Germany, there was greater pressure to keep all the people of northern Italy within the Catholic tradition. This meant trying once again to bring the mountain people of the Alps into its teaching and way of thinking. The northern Italian government heaped injustice and corruption upon these innocent people in an attempt to force them into "good" religious practices. The real issue was ultimately one of control: would the Waldensian population have the freedom to make their own behavioral choices, or would their choices be dictated from Rome via the northern Italian government? The methods for behavioral control varied from imprisonment, to confiscation of property, to the death sentence. A young couple were burned alive and their valuable farm was taken by the state for being caught having a private worship service while they were together alone in their own home. [83] Every appeal to the local governmental authorities for redress of their grievances against these injustices was ignored. Instead, they were systematically murdered for thinking independently of the majority and of the government. Finally they found themselves so opposed and oppressed that escape seemed to be the only way to survive. Traveling up over the Alps in heavy snow and cold, hundreds of people journeyed by foot into central and eventually northern Europe.

There they corresponded with the leadership and intellectuals of Europe, complaining about the injustice of intolerance. Shortly after this correspondence with the Waldensian people, we find these same European intellectuals producing the earliest writing on the subjection of toleration; on granting others the freedom to do what you think is wrong. The British author, philosopher, and politician John Locke (writing a couple of decades after his friends and colleagues met and corresponded with the Waldensian people) would be one of the loudest advocates for this kind of freedom and would suggest that any government that did not offer freedom to its subjects should be overthrown. It was in this thinking that our Western civilization developed with religion separated from the power of government and the government subject to the desires and vote of its population. [84]

There seems to be a direct chain from the Waldensian thirst for freedom to their communication with Europe about their plight, to the early ideas of intellectual and religious freedom, to the foundation of a free society in the West. In the deaths and injustices of the Waldensian people and other martyrs of their time were born the seeds of our freedom today. The deaths of these Italians were unfair and painful, but we are the beneficiaries. Their deaths bless us in that their pain is our education—and that is true of all pain.

We look at injustice today and see its horror. We recognize that the Rwandan genocide with its murder of people who were taller was repugnant and despicable. However, we humans have not always considered genocide to be tragic. Our current horror at the genocide practiced in Germany before and during World War II forgets that many Americans agreed with and supported genocide and other forms of discrimination during the early 1900s. We called it the eugenics movement: the study of genetics to improve the quality of the hereditary pool. The goal was to discourage those with defects or inheritable, undesirable traits from propagating and to encourage those with desirable qualities such as intelligence to reproduce. This movement had the support of some notable people of the time, including Theodore Roosevelt, Winston Churchill, and John Harvey Kellogg; the most infamous of the group was Adolf Hitler. [85]

Many Jews, Germans, Poles, Rwandans, and others like them died, proving the horrible reality that no human ought to die for any feature of their height, mental ability, race, or culture. This is a fundamental truth taught by their pain, even though it is not a popular truth. Still, millions of humans have not accepted this truth. Many in the Middle East refuse to openly disagree with the religious command to kill those who do not belong to their religion. [86] They also refuse to condemn the killing conducted by political organizations and other related organizations that murder civilians. The drug cartels and other gangs have never accepted this truth either. Nor have millions of people in the less-educated regions of the African and Asian continents. The idea that no one should die for being different is a minority belief if we consider the entire population of the world today.

Those of us who do accept that death is never to be inflicted on people for reasons that amount to discrimination seem content that only a few in this world accept it. We do not heartily promote this essential truth. We seem almost content that others die as long as it is not us here and now.

There are many other lessons we can learn from pain in this world. For example, we can learn the danger of arrogance. In past centuries, religion was one of the most significant influences in individual lives and in society. Religion had that influence because it was the method of searching for what we now call truth. Today, we have learned to trust science in our quest for truth. We trust science in part because science taught us to think that religion is arrogant when it is used to cover a mere human opinion being passed around as a profound truth due to the powerful position of the person expressing that opinion. While it is true that religion has preserved knowledge and provided meaning and context for us to understand our lives, truth has also been too often controlled by a few and tarnished by their mistakes.

When those purveyors of truth failed to examine the real world, when they concluded truth by careless examination of the available evidence and when they decided truth was determined by power rather than observation, they failed their responsibility. Science called the bluff of stale religion and brought observation back as a tool for understanding the real world. Now science is having some of the same problems as religion. A few people, through their influence, sometimes determine what we are taught as truth instead of confining all statements to disciplined observation. Sometimes power and money have more determination in finding truth than what has actually been ascertained

There are many more lessons to be learned from the suffering in this world. Moral clarity will come to us as we consider history (ancient and modern) and its lessons. The idea that suffering that is not a direct result of our own mistakes is actually part of a greater educational experience to identify and clarify moral truth is demonstrated in an old Bible story.

Job and the Meaning of Pain

Job is presented as a mega-farmer, business owner, and possibly town mayor. He apparently was a major economic, social, and political player of his time, connecting and influencing surrounding civilizations. His clothing and food industries may have supplied the contemporary Egyptian and Indus Valley civilizations through his camel-based business.

That is, Job was a major player in his era until a series of rapidly succeeding natural catastrophes put him out of business. Not only did he lose his livelihood, but he also lost all ten of his children and his health. Seeing as Job was the respected man that he was, he likely had many employees, possibly thousands, who depended on him for work. He may have also asked himself, "Who will take over my humanitarian work in the community?"

It is questionable whether or not anyone has suffered a greater injustice than Job did. The loss of his family, the destruction of his business, the suffering from sickness, the shame in his community, all the while being haunted by the meaninglessness of it all, caused Job to suffer on every human front. Yet in his agony, Job never let go of his love for God, his sanity, and his human decency. He never became hostile and hateful. From the beginning of his loss, Job accepted his misfortune with an elegance and flexibility that we can scarcely understand. He cried, but he didn't blame others. He agonized, but he didn't drift to fantasy to cope. He hurt, but he never attacked.

The book of the Bible that bears his name depicts a God who is engaged, sensitive, sympathetic, and interested in the welfare of Job as well as that of all humans, all the while arguing[87] with the devil himself. Satan, on the other hand, turns every suggestion of decency and nobility in Job into a cover for his own self-interest and greed. This devil injures Job almost beyond comprehension. God permits Satan to wreak his harm on Job with limitations, but God Himself never causes anyone harm. God makes his point by giving Satan enough rope to hang himself in letting the devil hurt loyal Job. This story demonstrates that God quietly suffers throughout human suffering. In the end, God rewards Job for his intense loyalty and decency. [88]

God wants only the service of love. He does not want us to obey Him out of dissatisfaction or anger. The only way we will love Him is if we can see for ourselves that what *He says* is good—is really good on its own merits—and that what *He says* is evil is intrinsically evil. Then we will trust that *everything* He says is good really is good, and *everything* He says is evil really is evil.

God's standard of good and bad need to be independently verified by our human experience. So long as we continue to accept and invest in evil (no matter how small or insignificant that evil) we perpetuate our moral disagreement with God and drive ourselves to stop trusting and loving Him.

Pain is the cost we all pay for God to make Himself vulnerably transparent to us, giving us the opportunity to appreciate Him. Pain is the cost we all pay to be able to learn moral truth in an immoral world. Pain is the price of investigating evil.

Sorrow is the major excuse we give for not embracing heaven. We think we are justified in acting like hell because we hurt. Job's example gives us no room to have a pouty pity party. Through his pain, which was only to reveal the truth of his unbribed loyalty to God, his character shone. His painful illustration was to show the whole world that the devil should change *his* actions or that the devil deserves to die for refusing to stop hurting all the rest of us.

Louis Slotin paid the price of the development of knowledge in his own untimely death. Job and the Italians of centuries gone by suffered for our good. They took hits for the team of humanity. Their pain was never in vain, for it provided us with a source of our knowledge.

One day, we will look back and realize that even the most apparently senseless pain was permitted by God to allow humanity to learn what is and isn't morality. Their unjust suffering is for the greater good of all humanity.

Does this mean we are just pawn pieces in a universal game of chess? Sometimes we are asked to suffer for no immediately discernible reason; does this suggest that God is a heartless and ruthless Being, just taking advantage of us for His own gain? Does allowing us to suffer in order for God to let us discover moral knowledge mean God has His—rather than our—best interest at heart?

Ask a high school chemistry teacher whether it is easier to do an experiment as a demonstration or to let her students do the experiment

Ask a parent who has taught his or her children to tie their shoes, "Which is easier, tying your child's shoe or letting your children learn to tie their shoes for themselves?"

If we let our children get burned mildly (just enough to say "ouch" and no more) to teach them to trust us when we say, "Do not touch a hot thing," are we being cruel and only looking out for our own good? It is far harder to silently suffer while you let someone else grow through mild suffering than to suffer yourself. Likewise, God experiences more pain from letting all the suffering occur that is necessary to garner moral knowledge than He ever would in any other way. His willingness to endure our suffering while He longs to protect and comfort us is proof of the depth of His love and not of the absence of it. It is not that we worship a God who does not have our best interest at heart, but that we love a God who has our best interest at heart so strongly that He is willing to suffer with and for us.

This is the point in Jesus' story about the prodigal son. Asking for the share of his inheritance early, the boy throws it all away in luxurious living. When he decides to return home, his father is waiting for him. Was the father cruel and calloused to let the boy make a point out of his own foolishness? One can merely imagine the suffering of that father until one has had children leave home under similar circumstances. But to those parents who have been given the special privilege of sharing in the experiences of God, we know it hurts more to let our children live fast and loose and wait for them to come home than it ever did to make our own mistakes.

You and I will suffer pain in our lives; some of that pain will be well deserved because of the consequences of our own actions. That pain is our teacher, for it "grows us up."

All of us will also suffer distress, pain, injustice, and agony that we do not deserve. It is our moment of Job. Take it for the team. Refuse to consider it personally. It isn't about you. It is for us. Let the rest of us learn from it. Get over it. Find your own purpose and mission in life. Find heaven for yourself. Never let pain keep you away from the joy, contentment, and success of heaven.

Getting over the pain we experience that we did not cause is just where we have difficulties. That is hard. And that is just where we need God. He suffered more injustice than any human ever will. Every one of us is unfair to God at some point. We hurt His heart. Many of us hurt His heart a lot. Yet God doesn't live in His pain. He is never obsessed with our unfairness to Him. He still sees us as friends. He still wants our company. He still wants us for His team. More than that, He looks past His pain to our pain because He loves us.

Our pain is His pain *also*. He cries when we cry. He is sympathetic to us. In that little sentence in the book of John it says very simply, "Jesus wept" (John 11:35). He wept all the way to the cross because of His compassion for us: "Surely he hath borne our griefs, and carried our sorrows" (Isaiah 53:4). He still weeps with us today, for He never changes.

What do we do with grief? We cannot avoid all of it. It is a reality in this world. The religion of Jesus is not an escape from pain, suffering, and sorrow. However, it does offer a way to handle and understand it.

In Matthew Chapter 9, Jesus provided comfort to a variety of people. He relieved the guilt of the palsied man. In a demonstration of His power to comfort the guilty heart through forgiveness, He then healed the man.

Later, He brought comfort to the anguished and embarrassed woman who had suffered from a blood disorder for years. She found healing in silent and inconspicuous contact with Jesus.

Then Jesus eased the pain of those who had lost their child through death by raising the church administrator's daughter back to life. Finally, Jesus comforted the blind men by returning sight to their eyes. His soothing acts were far more than a hug and a word of sympathy. They were so powerful that we almost forget that He was providing comfort.

In reading these people's history, let us find our own comfort. This same Jesus loves us and longs to help us. He wants to soothe us the way He comforted others so long ago. For many of us, when we ask, He will provide the same reassurance to us today that He gave people two millennia ago.

God may not always provide the comfort that we want or remove the source of pain, but He gives us the relief that we need. Paul tells us that he had this experience. In this we see that sometimes God lets us continue to suffer to keep us humble, literally.

"There was given to me a thorn in the flesh, the messenger of Satan to buffet me, lest I should be exalted above measure. For this thing I besought the Lord thrice, that it might depart from me. And he said unto me, My grace is sufficient for thee: for my strength is made perfect in weakness. Most gladly therefore will I rather glory in my infirmities, that the power of Christ may rest upon me. Therefore I take pleasure in infirmities, in reproaches, in necessities, in persecutions, in distresses for Christ's sake: for when I am weak, then am I strong" (2 Corinthians 12:7–10).

We have every right and privilege to find comfort and safety in God. When He chooses to permit us to suffer for our own good, we need to let that weakness be a chance for His strength to shine in and through us.

Sorrow and pain exist as side effects of the exploration of evil. Evil must be known to be intelligently rejected. And it must be intelligently rejected to choose good. Thus, no pain is in vain. All of it contributes to the universal comprehension of truth, even if it serves no good to the individual sufferer in the present moment.

Every tear drop is measured and appreciated by God. He has asked us to accept suffering with Him in order to reveal moral truths, but He always suffers more than we do. Let us appreciate His suffering. Let us be grateful that we can stand with Him and suffer for a greater cause. We must never let suffering distract us from God or heaven. It is never worth it. Instead, we should allow that pain to draw us into a closer, stronger, and more meaningful relationship with God.

The existence of suffering is an old argument used to reject the possibility of heaven. The dispute requires a good deal of humility from us as we respond. Too often humanity has failed to endure or even mitigate suffering and learn the moral lessons provided for us through it. Too often we have joined evil rather than permitting God to walk through the pain with us.

Nevertheless, suffering is not senseless. It has a moral and a value, however difficult it may be to accept this; and since it is not meaningless, it is not an argument against the reality and the possibility of heaven. Let us never abandon the blessings of heaven just because we have not yet personally found the sense, the value, in specific experiences of human suffering.

Chapter 8
THE CONCLUSION

Heaven Is for the Helpless

Heaven is available for everyone: the vulnerable, the helpless, the weak, the strong, and the rich. If heaven were only for the strong, the talented, the rich, or the beautiful, most of us would be left out. The glory of heaven is its availability to both the common and uncommon person.

That it is a fit for everyone is seemingly a problem. Whatever is good for everyone, generally, is good for nothing. Usually it is cheap and doesn't work. One size fits all is often a falsehood. The product generally fits no one very well.

Suppose we create an orchestra composed of just the common people. Invite anyone who works on Main Street to play the violin. Cello players can come from Front Street, viola players from Winding Way. For flute players, we accept anyone who lives on High Street. For French horns, we take anyone from Breezy Lane. What a group! Sally with thousands of hours of violin practice; Jim with none; Johnny just trying to make some noise. We now have hundreds of instrumentalists, and it doesn't seem to matter what anyone sounds like. We are an orchestra of everyone! How much do you think concert tickets will sell for?

We trust quality to come from the talented elite. A minority of excellent musicians makes a concert worth paying for. The more elite and exclusive the minority, the better the quality and the more impressive the experience will be. We appreciate; we admire; we pay for the work of a few great performers. Our appreciation of the excellence of a few demonstrates our certainty that we do not want to replace that excellence with the mediocrity of having everyone involved.

The same rule applies to art, business, sports, and the rest of life. Quality is the opposite of common.

We have an activity for everyone. Be the audience, a spectator, a body to fill the grandstand. It doesn't take a lot of skill to sit and watch a concert or a game or to yell at a television. Anyone can do it. We sacrifice our time and our money. We offer our devotion and our worship. We lose. The talented minority live at our expense.

So, in earthly matters, something for everyone is a losing proposition. To win typically means exclusion. Quality comes from rarity. Excluding anything but quality means only a few can be involved.

Why then is heaven for everyone? More importantly, does that make it cheap? Does heaven lose its quality when too many take advantage of the opportunity? Is it really open to anyone? Or is it just for losers?

Heaven is for winners because it *makes* winners out of losers. It is exclusive because it is exclusively for those willing to be changed from ordinary people into the elite. Heaven is for the rich, the powerful, the beautiful, the talented, and the strong because it imparts those qualities to we who do not measure up. It will make anyone strong who is willing to be transformed from his or her helplessly inferior condition. Let me give you a couple of examples.

Heaven Is for the Strong

Little room could be found to stand along the temple wall to watch the people coming together from far and near, size them up, and try to figure them out as they bustled about in preparation for the annual Passover feast. Farsi, Greek, Arabic, Amharic, Hebrew, and other languages immersed the observer in a cacophony. This was the heart of Israel, pulsating with the throngs of a national convention.

Aunt Lydia stood across the plaza; she had come from Phrygia, tired and anxious. The trip was long, her feet were sore, and her throat was thirsty, but Uncle John wouldn't find a room until a more urgent matter was finished. He wouldn't rest at all until they had found a sacrifice. He had to buy a lamb, young and innocent—no blemishes. It was hard shopping in the temple, but it was still better than wandering around Jerusalem trying to beat 20,000 other Jews to the bargain.

No one thought twice about purchasing the sacrifice on temple property. Ephesians bought their sacrifices in Diana's temple. Romans bought their sacrifices in Jupiter's temple. So naturally, Jews thought it was fine to buy their sacrifices in Jehovah's temple.

The tired lamb Uncle John found looked like what was needed, but the price was too high. All that money he had saved for a sacrifice, and then they couldn't afford it. A dove would have to do.

Look over there! Zacharias walked past, but he looked upset, as if he were complaining about the noise again; he was always complaining about the chaos being irreverent. Nearly everyone secretly agreed with him, but they wouldn't talk about it out loud, so no one would ever d anything about it. The politician-preachers made too much money to put a stop to the temple market. So everyone just put up with it.

Besides, it was so good to see Aunt Elizabeth and Uncle Alpheus. Cousin Lazarus was still full of stories. No doubt Mom and Aunt Joanna were swapping recipes, sorrows, and family news. Father and Simon had already started talking about religion, politics, and work. Boys talked about girls. Girls talked about boys as well as themselves. Kids ran around and played. Then we would all go home, happy that we were there, even if it was expensive and inconvenient and noisy.

This crowded spot in the temple courtyard was just as it always was that day. It was so good for family and friends to be surrounded by one another again.

Then it happened.

A Galilean strode through the gate. People whispered among themselves, "I've never seen Him. Have you?"

He stopped, stood in the courtyard, looked around at the fun, and took in the arguing, the haggling, the noise. His clothes indicated that He was a peasant. Still, something was different about Him. He stood erect, noble, like a king. His face changed.

Anger, authority, certainty, determination, power, and influence emanated from Him. He looked like He was in charge. He looked like He had complete control of Himself and of this place. He was too humble to be one of the preachers, too noble to be one of the politicians, too powerful to be one of the peasants. Who was this? Why did He look so determined, so stern, so angry, so incensed?

Everyone in the courtyard took notice. Every vendor, customer, and priest silently stared at the same Man. Business stopped. No one kept track of anything else. Everyone just stared at *the Man* on the steps.

He looked at each one, and His countenance was unique. No one had ever looked like that. No one had ever said so much with His face. *He looked into the heart of each individual.* People thought to themselves, *Does He know who I am? Can He read what I am thinking? Does He know that I cheated on my test last week? Does He know that I told my brother a fib so he wouldn't follow me into the temple? What does He know about me?*

This Man on the steps had the complete attention of everyone. Even the animals were quiet. The silence was painful, awkward, and unusual. No one knew what to do.

Finally, He spoke. Pointing to the animals, He ordered, "Take these things away." He articulated so authoritatively, so definitely, so firmly that people started running away. No one even stopped to think. The nation's most important businessmen, its top politicians, and all its temple vendors grabbed animals and left.

This was simply amazing. They had never obeyed anyone else's orders before. Leave their own capitol on the hill? Unthinkable! Impossible! One man told them to go. What? This was their place. They had spent years of education and networking to get here. They controlled this place. They were in charge, at least until that moment. The Man on the steps said, "Go." Not one powerful man thought of staying.

Something did stay. It has stayed down through the centuries, even to our own time. That is the memory of those moments. That memory, recorded in John 2:12–16, teaches us a lot about Jesus.

There was no campaign, no advertising, no gimmicks, no lecture, and no publicity. Jesus did not start His ministry with trying to stage healings. He did not win over the leaders of Israel with tact and influence. There were no presentations, no negotiations, no one-on-one meetings or back-room discussions. Jesus did not wait until He was popular. No. Jesus began with a big bang. He began by taking over Jerusalem and temporarily running it. He interrupted, just like Elijah did when he walked in before Ahab and told the king that there would be no more rain.

Jesus was assertive, even *courageous*. An unknown Galilean, maybe, but He fearlessly took on the nation's most powerful men. He demonstrated in one sentence that He was the universal Master of Ceremonies, *their* King; He was in control.

Just one look, one command: "Take these things hence."

That look, that sentence, took courage that most people don't have. We don't like noise in the chapel. We don't like injustice and extortion. We don't like clergy and politicians taking advantage of people. We don't like businessmen stealing or lying. We don't like religion failing people or science misguiding people. We don't like false hopes deceiving suicide bombers into murdering others. We don't like the world's injustice; we don't like its evil. We don't like those who perpetrate these things.

We don't like the chaos and confusion that is the result of evil in this world. Today, our noise and bustle are even louder than the Jewish world of 2,000 years ago. Many of us quietly stand by. We don't like it. We don't agree with it. Yet none has the courage to say, "Take all this away."

We remonstrate, we chide, we complain, but we don't demand. Jesus had the courage to order. It did not require a speech. He did not need to be fluent in any language. He did not need a degree. He did not need an introduction. All it took was one look and one sentence—He had the character and the courage for both.

Jesus is heaven in human form. He demonstrated heaven in the face of hell. While on earth, He was content, secure, and interested in the prosperity and happiness of every person. However, he did not tolerate our self-destruction, our hell. Heaven requires His kind of courage.

Over the pages of this book, you and I have explored a way to make ourselves better people. We have explored a way to find help from God, a method of fighting evil and making our families, our communities, and our world a better place. Incorporating the perspective and the actions we have discussed takes more character and courage than most, if not all, of us have.

This is exactly where we run into trouble. Not all of us will accept heaven. Many of you will turn Jesus down and throw away heaven, and you will do it for one of these reasons:

1. You will insist on the wrong heaven.

2. You will demand to be treated like heaven while you act like hell.

3. You will let hell cheat you right out of heaven.

Ditching Heaven for an Imposter

Many will throw away heaven because they want something cheaper, faster, and easier. They will go looking for the wrong heaven in that they will confuse their idea of what heaven should be—feeling good and experiencing comfort, convenience, and pleasure—with what heaven is. They will give up on excellence.

So they will look for heaven in the "right here" and the "right now." Some will look for heaven in the weather, in a spa, or in dark chocolate. Others will look for it on an island in the Caribbean, down in the ocean, or in a gambling town. Still others will look for it in hangin' out with friends or in sex. Those looking for heaven on earth will sweat and scheme and worry how to get enough money to buy heaven right here and right now.

All of this gratification put together still can never be called paradise. Rich people commit suicide. So do people living on a tropical island. Possibly the highest suicide rate in the world is among fifteen- to twenty-four-year-old boys in Micronesia, a nation of tropical islands. [89] Eating (even eating dark chocolate) apparently doesn't prevent suicide and exciting sex doesn't inoculate us against it either. Each of our earthly heavens eventually betrays us. Misery follows us from the beach to the mountain top, from the football game to the party. The loneliest place in the world is to be miserable while you are surrounded by a group of apparently happy people who don't seem to notice your sorrow. Joy doesn't come from our circumstances. Heaven is still something we experience inside, not something we merely find outside. Anyone searching for a cheap, quick "heaven" will miss the real one.

Let's stop blaming our circumstances and everyone else for what we experience. Let us personally take responsibility for *how* we experience it. We can choose our attitude, our goals, and our commitments. We can ask the Divine Invisible Being for His help and leading. We can battle against evil and be kind to all of our fellow humans. Whether or not we ever experience heaven depends on our choices, not our circumstances.

Squirrel Syndrome

Why do we throw away what is better for something less satisfying? Why do we chase the wrong heaven? Let me use what I call the *Squirrel Syndrome* to illustrate what happens. It seems a gray squirrel that I'll call Jack had wandered farther away than usual from his River Oak tree nest. Suddenly, his exploration was interrupted by the sound of a car. Jack's impulse to run from my noise for the comfort of his home tree became visible in his little body. His earnest look and the strain of his muscles showed confusion and fear, but running home meant running in front of the vehicle. The poor squirrel didn't know what to do. He ran back and forth over two feet of the paved highway trying to decide whether to run *to comfort* or run *away from danger*. I watched him turn around several times. Fortunately for Jack, he couldn't make up his mind. While he was running back and forth in the southbound lane, the car drove past in the northbound lane. Jack's indecision spared him to search for acorns another day.

Some of his cousins were not so fortunate. Temporarily, they found themselves safe where they were. Then they recognized the approach of danger and felt threatened. So they abandoned the safety of their locations to run to their favorite tree or to their long hidden stash of nuts. In choosing to *escape* the mere threat of danger, they ran right into *the path of death*. They failed to realize that running *toward* the comfortable and familiar may be the most dangerous course in the world. We then find their dead bodies as "road kill." This habit of running for something that looks at the moment to be the most convenient option, even if it kills you, is the Squirrel Syndrome.

Deer suffer from the Squirrel Syndrome also. Running back to the side of the road they want to reach, it does not occur to them that they have abandoned the safety they already enjoyed.

Humans can be afflicted with the same syndrome. Some will drink alcohol because it feels good. They even do it before they know they are going to drive because it feels good to drink. Waking up after the car crash never feels as good. They will choose the familiar and comfortable even though doing so puts their own lives and the lives of those around them at great risk.

Some would rather die a slow and painful death from cancer than give up on the temporary pleasure of a smoke before we get there. Still others will eat food that destroys their health because they like its flavor.

Millions will injure their lives and hurt their friends and family because they are more interested in doing what feels familiar and comfortable than in doing what is safe. They will run in front of the greatest dangers and let themselves die rather than choose the safety of something different. Many will pursue comfort even if it kills them. People may be smarter than the squirrel, but often they aren't wiser.

Every day most people work hard for a good life, putting in long hours at work or working a second job. They collect coupons. They go to school. They get involved in social organizations. They do all of this just to get as much satisfaction as they can collect.

Even after all their work and the use of all the intelligence they can muster, people have never created paradise on this earth. Most people still experience hardship. If they don't, millions of others do. Our world is a long way from heaven for everyone.

Our work to achieve heaven fails because we have the Squirrel Syndrome. We think of ways to run toward gratification rather than away from danger. We design and work for mediocrity and reject the real heaven in the process. We accept something that gratifies but does not satisfy us. We go for second-rate satisfaction in exchange for giving up on what we, in the depth of our souls, really want and long for with all of our hearts: a nurturing, harm-free society.

We may dedicate ourselves to living a life of leisure on a tropical island, but we are probably chasing pleasure rather than safety. If we demand respect from others that we have not earned and are unwilling to give them in return, we are chasing indulgence rather than safety. If we eat or drink something to feel good at the expense of health, we are seeking enjoyment but throwing away life. Heaven that is only outside of ourselves (rooted only in what we experience) may be pleasurable, but it is dangerous. Heaven that is a result of who we are (by the help of God), of our character, and our habit patterns, is safe.

The touching story of Aron Ralston is the opposite of the Squirrel Syndrome. He fell while on a hike in a national park. Alone in a canyon in Utah, he was dying of thirst and hunger because his right arm was jammed between an 800-pound rock and the canyon wall. Eventually, Aron made the difficult choice to cut off his own arm in order to live. [90] The sacrifice of the damaged part of himself in order to save his life is exactly what heaven requires. When the status quo is certain to end in suicide, let go of what is killing you. There is no reason to cut our right arm off under normal circumstances; but when his crushed right arm prevented Aron from having access to water, food, and a normal life, he gave up a part of himself.

This is exactly the issue. We have to give up a part of ourselves. Our selfishness, insolence, and intolerance all feel as much a part of us as our own right arm. But we cannot be heavenly and hang on to our selfish selves. We have to give up a part of who we are used to being.

Instead, we often abandon what we really want deep within ourselves because of what it requires giving up. Won't we let go of what seems normal and usual to get what is better? Ralston realized that sometimes this is a life-and-death question. Settling for the current status quo can really be committing suicide.

"Let's not pretend this is easier than it really is. If you want to live a morally pure life, here's what you have to do: You have to blind your right eye the moment you catch it in a lustful leer. You have to choose to live one-eyed or else be dumped on a moral trash pile. And you have to chop off your right hand the moment you notice it raised threateningly. Better a bloody stump than your entire being discarded for good in the dump" (Matthew 5:29, 30 *The Message*).

Ditching Heaven by Investing in Hell

Some of you will miss heaven, not because you look the wrong places, not because you settle for second rate. You will lose heaven because you insist on creating hell. You may be one of those who wants to plant hell and harvest heaven as a good return on your investment. We put hell in the pot and cook it, stir it, and season it. Then we expect to relish heaven out of our pot of hell.

This is a human problem. No matter how innocent we seem as babies, at some point we start treating others unkindly. How much hell we give to others depends on how much hell we have in our hearts, but all of us contribute at least a little to its existence. We yell at those whom we love most. We betray those closest to us. We shout, we get angry, we push, we whine, we manipulate, we sue, we report. We hurt others in the hopes that the pain we cause will make them treat us like heaven. Some of the worst examples of this kind of manipulation are seen in suicide bombings where random murderous actions are meant to terrorize society into yielding to unreasonable demands. Those who sponsor these suicide bombings think that heaven exists when society is subservient to *them*.

There are much less drastic examples of manipulation. Spouses and lovers indulge in smaller amounts of manipulation by choosing to nag and hurt each other just to get what they want out of the other. Parents intimidate their children into compliance. Bosses intimidate employees, and employees scare bosses into cooperation. These examples of manipulation may seem less dangerous than a suicide bombing, but they still wear away slowly on other people to make their lives painful, which may actually be more insidious.

The story is told of a runner who had run hundreds of miles. Someone asked him what caused him the most annoyance or bothered him most. Was it the height of the hills or the heat of the sun or the chilliness of the rain? The runner responded that the little stones in his shoes caused the most pain, or hell.

We constantly put little stones in our loved ones' shoes that really cause more accumulated pain than if we had done something grandly traumatic. Still, somehow we expect to excuse our own actions that hurt others while we hold them accountable for whatever stones they put in our shoes to hurt us. We expect that for all the misrepresentations and insults and hatred and frustration we exhibit toward others, they should give us respect and kindness and love. Having spent years putting hell on layaway and paying faithfully, we somehow expect to pick up our layaway, and it will be all heaven. This is selfishness.

Some of us really hold others to a higher standard of behavior than we will ever apply to ourselves. We expect them to always be kind and thoughtful to us, but we know that we will not always be kind and thoughtful toward them. We look at every issue to see how they can make us feel better, not how there can be a better world for all of us. Why don't we hold ourselves to the highest standard of behavior that we hold everyone else to? The famed Golden Rule is that we should *do* to everyone else according to the standard of treatment that we want to receive from them (see Matthew 7:12). It is not the un-Golden Rule we have replaced it with that is practiced by forcing everyone else to treat us by that same high standard of treatment while we hold ourselves to a lesser standard.

There is a better way. We can live like heaven even if we are surrounded by hell. We can receive hell and still give heaven. Jesus did it, and it worked. Chased and hated, threatened and falsely accused, Jesus was a constant fountain of blessing. He never complained. Joseph did it, and it worked. Betrayed and sold by his brothers, he gave those same brothers the best part of Egypt. Paul did it in prison, and it worked. Locked in the part of prison reserved for the worst criminals, he sang praises to God. While he was singing, an earthquake released him from prison. This better way has worked for me when I have tried it.

"Be not deceived; God is not mocked: for whatsoever a man soweth, that shall he also reap. For he that soweth to his flesh shall of the flesh reap corruption; but he that soweth to the Spirit shall of the Spirit reap life everlasting. And let us not be weary in well doing: for in due season we shall reap, if we faint not" (Galatians 6:7–9).

"Then shall the King say unto them on his right hand, Come, ye blessed of my Father, inherit the kingdom prepared for you from the foundation of the world: for I was an hungred, and ye gave me meat: I was thirsty, and ye gave me drink: I was a stranger, and ye took me in: naked, and ye clothed me: I was sick, and ye visited me: I was in prison, and ye came unto me. Then shall the righteous answer him, saying, Lord, when saw we thee an hungred, and fed thee? or thirsty, and gave thee drink? When saw we thee a stranger, and took thee in? or naked, and clothed thee? Or when saw we thee sick, or in prison, and came unto thee? And the King shall answer and say unto them, Verily I say unto you, Inasmuch as ye have done it unto one of the least of these my brethren, ye have done it unto me" (Matthew 25:34–40).

As one and then another contributes heaven to society, society becomes heavenly. Thus, *we create* heaven, for heaven exists when we create it, not when we receive it. We must live heavenly. We must have heaven in our hearts. Heaven is not just a place we might someday reach. It is first a choice we make, a choice to behave heavenly. *Heaven is a choice we make while we are living in hell.*

Heaven is to be thankful when we see the sun *and* when we feel the storm. It is to be thankful when our virtues are discovered *and* when our faults are uncovered so that we have the opportunity to improve. Heaven is the choice to be thoughtful to those who are kind to us *and* to be thoughtful to those who hurt us. It is the choice to refuse to let the treatment I receive from others affect the way I treat others. Heaven is the choice to trust God, to believe He is right and is taking care of me when I do not understand life and even when it hurts. It is the choice to be humble and grateful every day.

Heaven is that power provided so graciously by God to change my character, my behavior, and my desires. It is the power to be calm, content, circumspect, and gracious in every circumstance. It is the power to help others, no matter what circumstances we are living under. Heaven is the power to be *a useful member of society rather than to merely provide for my own comfort.*

"You're familiar with the old written law, 'Love your friend,' and its unwritten companion, 'Hate your enemy.' I'm challenging that. I'm telling you to love your enemies. Let them bring out the best in you, not the worst. When someone gives you a hard time, respond with the energies of prayer, for then you are working out of your true selves, your God-created selves. This is what God does. He gives his best—the sun to warm and the rain to nourish—to everyone, regardless: the good and bad, the nice and nasty. If all you do is love the lovable, do you expect a bonus? Anybody can do that. If you simply say hello to those who greet you, do you expect a medal? Any run-of-the-mill sinner does that.

"In a word, what I'm saying is, *Grow up.* You're kingdom subjects. Now live like it. Live out your God-created identity. Live generously and graciously toward others, the way God lives toward you" (Matthew 5:43–48 *The Message*).

Maybe you're thinking, *I don't have that character. I don't have the character to be kind to those who hurt me. I don't have what it takes to chase evil out of the temple like Jesus because He was God.* Think again. Jesus was God *and* man. Jesus is my *example. Christ*ians are *like* Christ. "My grace is sufficient for thee" (2 Corinthians 12:9).

Jesus' followers are also courageous. Elijah stood before Ahab. Three years later, he stood before all of Israel. Elijah felt like he was all alone in the fight against hell, and he fought the battle anyway (1 Kings 17:1–18:40). That took courage.

Moses fought against the hell of his time. Sometimes he seemed like the only one fighting against it. That took courage.

It took courage for Peter to stand in front of the same politicians who were behind the murder of Jesus and tell them to their face, "We ought to obey God rather than men" (Acts 5:29). It took courage for Paul to appeal to Agrippa until he almost became a Christian (Acts 25:13–26:28). And it took courage for Paul to continue to tell the story of Jesus after being beaten, imprisoned, shipwrecked, and stoned.

It took courage for Samuel to tell the people of Israel that they had made a wrong decision (see 1 Samuel 3:3–6). It took courage for Nathan to tell David that he had sinned (see 2 Samuel 12:1–14). With these events we have just begun. Heaven is for the strong: "for [God's] strength is made perfect in [human] weakness" (2 Corinthians 12:9).

It is for the strong because heaven requires the courage to face and conquer *yourself.* Samuel, Nathan, Elijah, Esther, Mary, Peter, and Martin Luther were all people of passions like ourselves. They were just sinners, but in Jesus they found the courage to face the evil in themselves and demand their own surrender to God. No one can ever demand that another person surrender his or her evil to God while the person making the demand is boasting of evil themselves.

Pseudo-Christians make the word "Christianity" stink by their attempt to control others. They do not have the courage to face themselves. If you do not have the courage to face the log in your own eye, do not curse the splinter in someone else's eye (see Matthew 7:3–5).

It took Jesus one look, one sentence to cleanse. If it takes you two sentences, watch out. Probably you are doing a work you should not do. Satan loves to use many sentences. He loves to deceive and manipulate. He loves to control and demand. He loves to throw his weight around. God doesn't waste His words. He never demands something from us that He will not do. He saved His words for healing, comforting, strengthening, teaching, confirming. His actions never disrespected the freedom and individuality of another. Learn from Him.

Never Let Hell Cheat You!

We do not live in heaven, and most of us do not have heaven inside. Thus, we live in hell, and the reason most of us live in hell is because we are distracted by hell. *We must never let hell cheat us out of heaven.*

Distraction is easy. As a child, I loved distractions. When I started school, I paid so much attention to the other students that I had trouble finishing my own work. As a student of heaven, I still have the same trouble. It is a lesson subtly hinted at in one of Jesus' parables found in Matthew 13:47–50:

> "Again, the kingdom of heaven is like unto a net that was cast into the sea, and gathered of every kind: which, when it was full, they drew to shore, and sat down, and gathered the good into vessels, but cast the bad away. So shall it be at the end of the world: the angels shall come forth, and sever the wicked from among the just, and shall cast them into the furnace of fire: there shall be wailing and gnashing of teeth."

Here, Jesus clearly taught us that not everyone who seems or professes to love God actually does. There are good fish and bad fish. There is a related problem, however, that isn't so obvious. We are almost all sure we are one of the really good fish, so we settle in to find out who is bad. In fact, we are generally so busy watching the other fish that we don't ever become a really good one ourselves.

Has your spouse cheated on you? Has your mother mistreated you? Has your child embarrassed you? These experiences are no excuse for ever hurting anyone—your spouse, your mother, your child, or anyone else—in a spirit of revenge.

Has your church disappointed you? Have your friends let you down? Did your boss take advantage of you? Don't hurt them back just to get revenge.

Do you have a painful life? Is hell busy sucking you into its belly? Do you feel like life is unfair? Do you feel like God isn't giving you enough comfort? When life isn't fair, the injustice we suffer is an explanation of why we hurt, *not an excuse to hurt someone else.*

Do you need more money, more friends, more comfort, more justice? Have you let hell take away your heaven?

How your boss, your spouse, your child, or your friends treat you should never change you negatively. You should be content and grateful when the sun shines and when it rains. Never let hell become your excuse for missing heaven.

People throw heaven away all the time. The biggest excuse they use is this: "Hell happened to me." We are rude because we are stressed. We neglect family and friends because life is hard. We abandon God because we experience injustice and hypocrisy. We are distracted by hell. We live in hell. We are surrounded by hell. Those are our reasons for rejecting heaven.

So let me remind you that hell is never good enough to replace heaven. Hell is never worth enough to let it cheat you out of heaven. Let go of hell. Give it up. Forget about it. Remember, we have to choose heaven while we are in hell. So never let hell be your excuse. Your father, your mother, your brothers, your sisters, your wife, your husband, your boss, your neighbor are never more important than heaven.

Heaven is here. Jesus said so. "Repent, because heaven is here." (Matthew 4:17, paraphrased). Will we accept Jesus' words? Or will we let the weather or our family or some injustice or some unrealized ambition convince us to live in hell? The power and wisdom of heaven are available to us right now. All we need to do is ask (see Matthew 7:7).

Furthermore, we should never settle for a false heaven. Heaven isn't a one-way street of blessings coming our way. We shouldn't let any power of hell steal heaven from living within us. Hell couldn't conquer Jesus. Let us ask for His help so that it doesn't conquer us either! Don't act like that.

In addition we all too often reject heaven because we refuse pain. Pain is in the doorway to heaven. We cannot escape it. We can find heaven beyond it if we only keeping moving forward by the help of the Divine Invisible Being.

Heaven Accepts No Excuses

Heaven tolerates no excuses. No one can have heaven and make any excuses at the same time. Excuses are the building blocks of hell. The difference between heaven and hell is whether or not we make excuses. Those who are honest enough in their own hearts and minds to face their life will have heaven, even if it hides behind the cloud a little while. Those who make excuses cannot have heaven (see

Matthew 7:21–23), for any excuse would ruin heaven. Excuses always attempt to shift the blame away from the cause, especially when the cause is found in ourselves. They do not allow us to accept liability for our own misdeeds, making problems and issues impossible to resolve. They destroy relationships and ruin careers and lives.

When we refuse to make any excuse, responsibility is then appropriately placed on the source or the cause. Then any misunderstandings can be resolved. Wrongs can be admitted and made right. Heaven exists in our hearts when we live in a world of no excuses.

Heaven Is for the Weakest

If you do not have the courage heaven requires, then you are not alone. I am weak. You are weak. We are all weak. We are all sinners. Thank God, heaven is just for us who are weak.

David seemed weak. He moved from one hideout to another. He was an outcast, alone. Slowly family and friends joined him. As the days moved past, more gathered to join Israel's most trusted reject. When life seemed unfair under Saul, people joined David (see 1 Samuel 22:1, 2). Among those hundreds, a few distinguished themselves. These were valiant soldiers. They were part of the team who fought with David. They were his friends when he seemed to have none. They were his servants when all he seemed to have were enemies. They were loyal, when all seemed to be against him. They stuck with him, whatever happened, and David stuck with them. (See 1 Samuel 23:1–24:22.)

Shortly after Saul's death, both Judah and Israel crowned David as their king (see 2 Samuel 2:4; 5:3). Slowly he became very powerful. So David took his loyal friends along with him as the new administration (see 2 Samuel 2:3). Israel relaxed under the prosperity of the Davidic reign. David's friends found houses in Jerusalem and settled down.

Uriah was one of the most loyal and special of those friends. He found a house near the palace. Why shouldn't he? Uriah was (according to 1 Chronicles 11:10 & 41) one of the king's most trusted men. He got married. Then, when Israel went to war again, Uriah went with them. He was a disciplined man, one of the army's best. He was a trusted soldier, a hero. Joab and David relied on him. After all, Uriah had risked his life with them.

Then David saw Uriah's wife. Oh, was she beautiful! David slept with her and she became pregnant. Since she was already married, King David killed her husband to cover up the pregnancy. David ordered the death of one of Israel's bravest and finest men, just to hide his own adultery with Uriah's gorgeous wife. (See 2 Samuel 11:1–17).

In his early life, David demonstrated great personal strength of character, even when he seemed less than powerful in the nation. When David killed Goliath, he was morally strong (see 1 Samuel 17:48–51). When David would not kill Saul while the king slept in the cave, David was strong in character (see 1 Samuel 24:1–12). When David mourned the death of Abner, he was also strong. But prosperity weakens any of us. The more we prosper, the weaker we are likely to be. Poverty and hardship strengthen our characters (James 1:2–4). They made David strong. Prosperity, on the other hand, made David weak.

Before his moral failing, David had to ask around to find whose wife this exquisite lady was. When he heard that she was Uriah's wife, David knew well who he was. Yet David was too weak with passion to save the life of someone he knew. Sex and pleasure meant more to him than the life of any of his employees or even his own close friend. Heaven was just what weak David needed most. Listen to the prayer of David as a weak sinner:

> "Have mercy upon me, O God, according to thy lovingkindness: according unto the multitude of thy tender mercies blot out my transgressions. Wash me thoroughly from mine iniquity, and cleanse me from my sin. For I acknowledge my transgressions: and my sin is ever before me. Against thee, thee only, have I sinned, and done this evil in thy sight: that thou mightest be justified when thou speakest, and be clear when thou judgest. Behold, I was shapen in iniquity; and in sin did my mother conceive me. Behold, thou desirest truth in the inward parts: and in the hidden part thou shalt make me to know wisdom. Purge me with hyssop, and I shall be clean: wash me, and I shall be whiter than snow. Make me to hear joy and gladness; that the bones which thou hast broken may rejoice. Hide thy face from my sins, and blot out all mine iniquities. Create in me a clean heart, O God; and renew a right spirit within me. Cast me not away from thy presence; and take not thy holy spirit from me. Restore unto me the joy of thy salvation; and uphold me with thy free spirit. Then will I teach transgressors thy ways; and sinners shall be converted unto thee. Deliver me from bloodguiltiness, O God, thou God of my salvation: and my tongue shall sing aloud of thy righteousness. O Lord, open

thou my lips; and my mouth shall shew forth thy praise. For thou desirest not sacrifice; else would I give it: thou delightest not in burnt offering" (Psalm 51:1–16).

Heaven Is What Makes the Weak Strong

Jonah in the belly of the whale was a weak man (Jonah 1:17–2:10). Mary, when Jesus cast seven devils out of her, was a weak woman (Mark 16:9). The woman caught in adultery was a weak woman (John 8:3–11). The man let down through the roof, knowing his own sin was the cause of his sickness, was a weak man (Mark 2:4, 5). The repentant thief on the cross was a weak man (Luke 23:39–43). Jesus still loves to help weak men and weak women. Heaven is just for us who are weak. In fact, "the gospel of Christ … is the *power* of God unto salvation to every one that believeth" (Romans 1:16, emphasis added).

> "As many as received him, to them gave he *power* to become the sons of God, even to them that believe on his name: which were born, not of blood, nor of the will of the flesh, nor of the will of man, but of God" (John 1:12, 13, emphasis added).

I have never met a totally strong or totally weak person. Elijah stood on Carmel one day and ran from Jezebel the next. David faced Goliath one year and fell the victim to sex another. "For what I do is not the good thing that I desire to do; but the evil thing that I desire not to do, is what I constantly do" (Romans 7:19 *Weymouth New Testament*).

Intellectual and spiritual power, a perception of what is right, and a desire for goodness exist in every human heart. Against these principles there is struggling and an antagonistic power. Each of us has experienced good and evil appealing to our minds and succeeding in our lives. There is in our human nature a tendency toward evil, a force we cannot resist. Only one Power can withstand this force and allow us to reach the ideal that in our innermost soul we know to be the only satisfying one. We can find help in only that Power—Jesus. Cooperation with Him is man's greatest need.

We are born as a house divided against itself. We are born strong and weak at the same time. Through the sorrows and challenges of life, if we turn to God, we can become strong in Him. His strength is made perfect in remedying our weakness—that is heaven.

We are weak, alone, and helpless. Heaven hasn't made me rich, powerful, or famous. It never gave me back my family that deserted me or the friends that rejected me. It never took my daily struggle away. It is changing me. It is strengthening me each day. Heaven has provided the power to forgive.

As I have experienced, when we have heaven within us, we have the power to be patient. We have the power to be cheerful. We have the power to keep going. We have the power to stand when all around us is falling. We have the power to listen when all around us is confusion. We have the power to be content when all around us is discontent. Heaven makes us strong. It found us when we were weak, and it saves us. Heaven is creating in us the characters it demands of us. The changes that heaven is making in me are the most satisfying accomplishment I've ever experienced. Thank God for heaven!

Chapter 9
HEAVEN IS YOURS

Why Didn't I Find It?

"Daddy, I can't find it." As daddy's new assistant, my first report to the family CEO was rather bleak. "I can't find your hammer, Daddy."

Maybe it was the bright red-and-black handle or the silvery head. Whatever it was, I always thought of that specific hammer as *my father's hammer*. That is the hammer I looked for that sunny morning when my father asked me to go get it. That is the hammer I couldn't find.

My father had other hammers. That day he wanted another hammer, the one that had only a black handle, but my four-year-old eyes didn't see it because I was still looking for that distinctive red-and-black handle. It didn't matter how many things I saw. As long as I didn't see *that* hammer, I couldn't find any hammer.

I don't know how many times over the years I had to go back and tell my father that I couldn't find whatever *it* was. Many of those times he patiently went looking with me. Often the tool was right under my nose, but my young eyes weren't used to finding those tools in a different place or with a different color or texture than I was used to seeing. Until experience trained me to see what was in front of me, there were many things I could never find.

As an adult, I've seen that childhood experience repeated many times. Things have happened right in front of me, and I needed more experience to "see" what I was seeing. I've seen friends who had deep emotional pain eating their hearts out like it was strong acid. Later, I would look back and see that they were crying out all along, and I was blind to the view in front of my nose.

But my blindness isn't always about pain. My children surprise me with artistic talents and logical skills that I didn't see in them at first. Only experience has opened my eyes.

Heaven doesn't seem any different to me. I've spent years looking for it, working for it, longing for it, only to find out that *heaven really is here*. It was here all along. I was looking at it. I just didn't know how to recognize what I was seeing. I didn't know how to experience what was in front of me.

I hope that in our journey together over the pages of this book, you have had a glimpse of what heaven can be while we are still here on this earth. I hope your eyes are open to what is around you right now.

Heaven Is For You

We started with a definition of heaven after we looked at heaven's absence in our lives. Most of us look every day, but we haven't found what we are looking for. Then I told you that heaven is right here. This heaven is not a place you go to someday; it is your attitude each day. It is hearing God and depending on Him. It is changing your habits and ideas with His help. It is fighting evil and winning. It is being kind to all God's creatures. It is enjoying pleasure without indulging in anything that will hurt ourselves or anyone else. It is hearing the message of pain intelligently without being distracted by the existence of that pain. It is pursuing this lifestyle consistently and relentlessly.

Heaven is not any one of these things by themselves. It is the whole package lived every day of our lives. Heaven is chosen, not found. Heaven is made, not discovered. Heaven is living our lives by a particular standard—God's—all the time.

This heaven requires hard work, but hard work does not earn it. Hard work does not bribe God into giving it. Hard work commits us to it, even when cheap alternatives try to distract us. Hard work keeps us loyal to it when we are tempted to quit. Hard work implements it when things are easy and when they are not.

So I invite you to choose heaven with me. The choice I am suggesting is not something out of spontaneous curiosity only. It is a choice to commit ourselves to this fight as long as we have breath. It is a choice to seek our welfare and that of every other person simultaneously. It is a choice to live life nobly and to reject anything, however comfortable it feels or however attractive it seems, that falls short. It is the choice to live more nobly than our circumstances. It is a choice to be heaven revealed in human flesh.

I invite you because I cannot make you accept heaven. We tear the beauty and joy from heaven if anyone ever uses force, manipulation, or deceit. We just can't use the tools of hell to promote heaven.

Even so, I can promise that heaven is, and always will be, more satisfying than any alternative. The joy of heaven kept Jesus focused on sharing it even when treated as a criminal and then murdered. The contentment of heaven kept thousands of people dedicated and loyal to it even when others cut them in pieces, burned them, or tore them apart. Heaven can keep you humble, purposeful, and generous when life smiles upon you. Heaven can keep you calm, thoughtful, considerate, and focused when life attacks you. Heaven, and the only God who provides it, offers the one viable solution to our hell. Other things may help us cope for a little while. They may help us survive, but nothing else will ever take hell away from every person all the time as heaven does.

At the beginning of this book, I suggested that we can find heaven revealed in humanity's most difficult moments. It is counterintuitive to do so. We want to find heaven in our most comfortable moments. Like the squirrel, we want to go for the familiar even when it hurts us. I hope you have come to agree with me over these pages that there is a better life right now than the status quo. I hope you have found, even looking into the hardest moments of human life, a contentment, joy, and peace that are more than worth the effort of searching.

There is a heaven in the future with every benefit we can imagine and many benefits that are beyond our imagination. There is a more glorious life available in the future. I hope you have had a chance to see that the glory of the future begins in the daily choices of the present. I hope you have seen how fulfilling life can be right now if we only ask our Heavenly Father for help in moving the stones that are in our way.

I looked for an example that summed up this book. I can't find any other better than Jesus.

He was social, stepping out of His "comfort zone" to befriend others. He nourished His relationships. He firmly, rationally, and in a dignified way confronted the most dangerous of evils in society. He maintained a cheerful attitude and constantly communicated with His Father. He lived a life of service mixed with joy and heartache, pleasure and grief. He had many pleasures, but those pleasures never injured anyone. Jesus is heaven in real life. He shows us how to choose the best attitude in every moment, how to make the best of every circumstance. He shows us how to accept God and depend on Him. He shows us how to persistently, benevolently, consistently oppose everything that is evil. He shows us how to give others the kind of relationship we want to receive. He lived heaven in a different time and culture. He is challenging you and me to do the same now and in our own cultures. He offers us heaven.

What are we going to do with this gift that Jesus gave us? It cost Him too much for us to throw it away. That would not be right. No, it would just be mean to give Jesus hell in exchange for Him giving me heaven. I refuse to do that. What about you?

I'll take heaven! Yet it won't be paradise if I keep it all to myself. Now it is *your* turn to embrace it and pass it on to others. May God bless you as you do so.

ENDNOTES

1   Rudyard Kipling, "The Stranger," Poetry Lovers Page, http://www.poetrylover-spage.com/poets/kipling/stranger.html (accessed February 4, 2014).

2   A. Jay Adler, "I Am a Man: When American Indians Were Recognized as People Under US Law," The Sad Red Earth, July 7, 2012, http://sadredearth.com/i-am-a-man-when-american-indians-were-recognized-as-people-under-u-s-law/ (accessed February 4, 2014).

3   "Bathyscaphe *Trieste*," Wikipedia: The Free Encyclopedia, http://en.wikipedia.org/wiki/Bathyscaphe_Trieste (accessed February 4, 2014).

4   Bill Chappell, "Descending Into the Mariana Trench: James Cameron's Odyssey," The Two-way, Breaking News from NPR, May 23, 2013, http://www.npr.org/blogs/thetwo-way/2013/05/23/186302916/Mariana-Trench (accessed February 5, 2014).

5   "What is the difference in elevation between the Mariana Trench and Mount Everest?" Answers, http://wiki.answers.com/Q/What_is_the_difference_in_elevation_between_the_Mariana_Trench_and_Mount_Everest?#slide=1 (accessed February 4, 2014).

6   "To the Moon and Beyond: Neil Armstrong and Buzz Aldrin," The Greatest Adventures of All Time, *Time Lists*, http://content.time.com/time/specials/packages/article/0,28804,1981290_1981366_1981789,00.html (accessed February 5, 2014).

7   "The Telescope: Hubble Essentials," HubbleSite, http://hubblesite.org/the_telescope/hubble_essentials/image.php?image=launch (accessed February 5, 2014).

8   "Life and Work," Viktor Frankl Institute, http://www.viktorfrankl.org/e/lifeandwork.html (accessed February 6, 2014).

9   See Luke 2:1–7 and Matthew 2:1–18 for some of the childhood difficulties Jesus experienced. John 7:2–5 gives us a glimpse of the relationship between Jesus and his brothers. See Matthew 22:15–18; Mark 3:22, 30; John 8:6 for some examples of the abusive attitude of some people toward Jesus.

10   Three attempts in one weekend: (1) John 7:30; 44-53; (2) John 8:59 (these may well have been the stones in the temple they expected to use to stone the helpless women mentioned earlier in the same chapter); and (3) John 10:31, 33, 39. Betrayal: see Matthew 26:47–50. Death: see Matthew 26:57–27:50.

11   The conversation is recorded in Luke 17:20, 21. The kingdom of heaven is an esoteric term. We do not use it much anymore. We don't say the kingdom of Spain, the kingdom of France, or the kingdom of the United States of America. We shorten it. Let us recognize the term for heaven the same way we would recognize another country: heaven—not the kingdom of heaven, just plain and simple heaven.

12 For example, Jesus taught that private prayer (Matthew 6:5, 6), private charity, (Matthew 6:1–4), and private fasting (Matthew 6:16–18) were the quiet ways to produce public spiritual results. He insisted that humans should be free from anger (Matthew 5:22), free from any thought of sex outside of marriage (Matthew 5:28–30), and from any infidelity in marriage (Matthew 5:32). He taught us to have communication so meaningful and clear that we did not need to refer to any external support to prove our credibility (Matthew 5:34–37). He taught us to be so tough-minded and disciplined (Matthew 5:20; John 2:14-16 and other passages that are necessary to contextually appreciate the next point from Matthew 5:38-48) that we would not be taken advantage of easily. He also taught us to be so filled with goodwill and a willingness to work with others (Matthew 5:38-48) that any relationship issue could be resolved should the other side show the least willingness.

13 Matthew 13:24–30.

14 See Matthew 6:33; 12:28; 13:11, 24–33, 36–53; 18:23–35; 25:1–13; John 3:1–8; consider also Romans 14:17.

15 Matthew 5:10 (compare with verse 5); 7:21-23; 25:34; Luke 22:18

16 In Mark 10:30 Jesus talked of "eternal life" in the world to come, using the phrase as we are more accustomed to hearing it used. But in John 6:54 Jesus speaks of having "eternal life" here and now. John 10:28 at first glance seems ambiguous, but in John 11:25, 26 Jesus spoke of life as being the same as trust in God. He referred to those who were dead before they became alive by trusting God. Then He promised "eternal life" to those who believe in Him. In John 17:2, 3, Jesus again noted "eternal life" as present on earth already and being synonymous with knowing God. The apostle John talked of "eternal life" already existing inside the believer in 1 John 3:15; 5:13. He also affirmed once again that "eternal life" is to know God in 1 John 5:20. Also, Paul wrote that "the wages of sin is death but the gift of God is 'eternal life'" (not merely the hope of "eternal life" but the reality of it) in Romans 6:23.

17 Note that for Jesus, centuries ago, the primary meaning He gave was character and power. But the primary meaning His listeners gave was experience and location. Many of my readers may misunderstand the meaning of the word "heaven" as I use it. If Jesus in three years of teaching and thirty-three years of living did not overcome the misunderstanding of His listeners, there is not much hope for someone so inferior in character and ability to communicate as I am. But He did the best that could be done, even though He knew the limitations of His effort. I can only follow His example and hope that you understand the subject better for my efforts.

18 For the theologians reading this who wonder why mention "asking" when salvation is a free gift accepted as we trust God, let it be noted that the Pauline epistle that most clearly gives us the idea of salvation as a gift is the one that expresses our need of asking equally blatantly. After establishing the truth that God's blessing cannot be earned in the earliest chapters of Romans, Paul addresses the apparent incongruency with his message to his immediate audience of being surrounded by Jews that claimed to be God's people without trusting Him; that is to claim to have exclusive right to God's greatest blessing by a combination of having the right genes and working for it. He faults these Jews for not having the greatest

of God's blessings (9:31) because they did not trust God to give His blessings to them (9:32) and did not submit to Him but rather created their own pretense to replace what God offers (10:3). He goes on to argue logically from the discussion of human transparency before God given in Psalms 139 for complete authenticity in our relationship to God. He presents this authenticity as manifested by our dependence on God (quoting Isaiah 28:16 cf Isaiah 49:23) and our personal appeal to God (quoting Joel 2:32). (The quotation from Joel is the more interesting. It comes at the climax of a prophecy of great disaster. The concept of calling upon God is introduced as the course of action in times of terrible distress. This context gives added depth to the meaning of the word "call." Peter quoted and applied this prophecy to his time some two thousand years ago (Acts 2 especially verse 21). Peter's quotation also increases the importance of this concept of "calling.") Paul then argues on the basis of the idea that one who calls on God must already trust Him, as we only appeal to those we believe could at least possibly help (Romans 10:14, 15). Therefore, Paul apparently holds the fellow Jews of his day accountable for missing the essential blessing of God, given to those who are authentic in their religion, because they did not "call" upon Him (considering that this "call" includes the reality of faith).

I have simply used a more common modern word, "ask," for this Pauline essence of "accepting" the blessing of God, which he called the gospel. In doing so, I have relied on the Pauline conception of this "asking" or "calling" as the incorporation of faith in God and repentance toward God. I have also relied on the Pauline conception that this "asking" is a response to the approach of the Divine to our souls and never an act initiated by us before God appeals to us. Here Paul uses asking as an important protection for our freewill, revealing a loving God unwilling to force Himself upon those who do not explicitly express or "ask" for His help, and never as a work by which we earn God's favor. (Compare chapter 9, where Paul argues that the freewill of God is insulted by formalism and chapter 8 where he presents God as having prepared everything for our salvation, making our freewill the only thing that can prevent that salvation from occurring.)

Jesus uses the very word "ask" as His own expression of how we are to cooperate in receiving the great outpouring of grace in Luke 11:5-13. He, too, presents asking as the appropriate means of demonstrating that the reception of grace doesn't come under duress but is the choice of free will. Nothing in the parable suggests that we ask in order to earn salvation or any other blessing that God offers.

Jesus uses a variant of this same advice in His greatest manifesto of His mission on earth. After the introduction of blessing and exposé of the moral failing of that time in the fifth chapter of Matthew, Jesus introduces the way of success with God to be a private religion that has great public results in chapter six. In chapter seven, He begins with a warning about religious extremism and then comes to His conclusion. His conclusion focuses on how to obtain the morality He announced and the importance of actually obtaining it. Thus, verses 7–11 are the heart of Jesus' gospel message, the explanation of how to be moral. And these verses are an explanation of how to "ask" God for His moral strength and wisdom.

Since Jesus and Paul consider the gospel to be a cooperation between God and a human, both of whom have free will, that occurs when God's offer and the human's request are exchanged, I think we are on safe ground to use the word "ask" as an explanation of our part in cooperation with God.

A number of Jesus' healings confirm this. Take a few examples: Mark 1:40, 41; Luke 17:11–19; 18:35–43. In yet another healing of body and soul, it is plainly stated that Jesus had the healing power available to heal the body and soul of every person present. The grudging religious delegates from the various Jewish churches were unwilling to respond to the grace Jesus offered. But a man with a serious, debilitating sickness responded to that offer of grace. He was so anxious to respond that his friends skipped the impossible crowds and let him down through the roof. (They would have never have gone to such work and risked the anger of the homeowner if the sick man was not seriously interested in being healed by Jesus.) The action was enough of a plea for help, a "calling" upon the mercy of God, that Jesus answered before a word was actually spoken.

From the last story, we can conclude that "asking" God can be done through sincere and heartfelt words or through actions. God responds to us, as He told the helpless intruder of 2,000 years ago, "Your sins [or evil is] are forgiven you" (Mark 2:5), anytime we demonstrate an attitude of asking.

Expressing our way of accepting all of Jesus' gift to us as asking is no expression of human works. He motivates our request. He puts on display His own love, compassion, and terrible power, suggesting the value of the request. No human can ever honestly claim to initiate the divine relationship by asking God for anything. But every divine-human relationship that has ever existed can accurately be said to have started by some form of word or act expressing the need of the human for all the blessings that God offers each of us. We literally receive heaven just by asking for it.

19 Matthew 9:13; 12:41; 21:29; Mark 2:17; compare also Matthew 13:45, 46.

20 See Romans 14:17 again.

21 Daniel 6:7. Interestingly, Daniel is listed as the most important of the "Presidents" of Medo-Persia in verse 2. By claiming in verse 7 that "all" of the presidents consulted together, these sly governmental representatives asserted that Daniel had been consulted and that he had agreed. They used his name against him.

22 Matthew 7:16-20.

23 John 16:2.

24 Matthew 25:31-46.

25 Proverbs 16:18-20; 18:12.

26 Matthew 5:44, 45; Romans 12:20, 21.

27 My mother's attitude toward me softened as she aged. It would be unfair to fact to say that the moment I witnessed those tears was the moment of change. She gradually became less hostile and eventually even appeared accepting and kind in some of our last conversations. But those tears were the first and only positive emotional expression I ever received from my mother.

28 I've paraphrased this passage.

29 "George Mueller, Orphanages Built by Prayer," Christianity.com, http://www.christianity.com/church/church-history/church-history-for-kids/george-mueller-orphanages-built-by-prayer-11634869.html (accessed February 25, 2014).

30 Fred Barlow, "Robert Moffat: Missionary," Missionary Biographies, Worldwide Missions, http://www.wholesomewords.org/missions/bmoffat.html (accessed February 25, 2014).

31 "William Wilberforce (1759–1833): The Politician," The Abolition Project, http://abolition.e2bn.org/people_24.html (accessed February 25, 2014).

32 This statement is not meant to discount prophecy. Rather, it is descriptive of the historical passages of the Bible. The point is simply that the Bible primarily discusses the culture, issues, problems, joys, and success of bygone millennia. We are expected to learn by comparison to our present circumstances.

33 I've given an approximate translation of the German proverb: "Ein schönes Gesicht ist nicht jedem gegeben; doch ein freundliches Gesicht können wir alle machen."

34 Revelation 21:8.

35 Jamie Glazov, "Martyred in the USSR, Militant Atheism in the Former Soviet Union," Frontpage Mag, http://www.frontpagemag.com/2013/jamie-glazov/martyred-in-the-ussr-militant-atheism-in-the-former-soviet-union/ (accessed February 26, 2014).

36 Steve Newcomb, "Five Hundred Years of Injustice," http://ili.nativeweb.org/sdrm_art.html (accessed February 26, 2014).

37 "The African Slave Trade and the Middle Passage," The Terrible Transformation, http://www.pbs.org/wgbh/aia/part1/1narr4.html (accessed February 26, 2014).

38 "Genocide in the 20th Century: The Nazi Holocaust 1938–1945," The History Place, http://www.historyplace.com/worldhistory/genocide/holocaust.htm (accessed February 26, 2014).

39 Jesus stated as much in Matthew 7:16–20. While He expressed this axiomatic law in relation to detecting deceptive clergy, He did so clearly meaning for us to take a universal truth and apply it to the specific circumstance under discussion. His broader point was that our actions (which He called fruits) are the consequence of who we are (that is, our character). Jesus restated this in different circumstances in Matthew 15:19, 20 (also recorded in Mark 7:20–23). Jesus maintained that any person whose thoughts were free from evil would be a person whose actions were free from evil.

40 See the beginning of Chapter 3: Getting Heaven.

41 2 Corinthians 10:12.

42 "Genocide in Rwanda," United Human Rights Council, http://www.unitedhumanrights.org/genocide/genocide_in_rwanda.htm (accessed February 26, 2014).

43 Mukahirwa Stephanie as told to J. P. Cruz, "Healing a Broken Heart," The Reformation Herald, vol. 49, no. 2, http://www.sdarm.org/files/publications/periodicals/rmrh/pdf/rmrh2008_2_en.pdf (accessed February 26, 2014).

44 Vengeance biblically belongs to the Lord (Deuteronomy 32:35, 43; Psalm 94:1; Isaiah 35:4; 59:14–17; 61:2; 63:4; Micah 5:15; Nahum 1:2; Romans 12:19; Hebrews 10:30, 31). This does not mean that we no longer value vengeance. It means that we trust God and appreciate Him for doing it better than we can (see Psalm 58:10, 11; Jeremiah 11:20; 20:12). Psalm 149:5–9 goes so far as to express humans carrying out a vengeance that is pleasing to God. Only a fanatic would consider this as any justification for violence as the Bible is clear that those who trust God do not offer any violence for their own protection or to advance their own goals (Matthew 5:39–41; 26:52, 53).

45 This concept of forgiveness bringing active consequences of compassion, gratitude, and love occurs throughout the Bible. For example, compare the twin brothers, Esau and Jacob, meeting after several years of separation. That separation was caused by the behavior of each one of them, especially the manipulative dishonesty of Jacob. Both brothers cried in sorrow for the past (Genesis 27:34, 38; 32:9–11). Their sorrow was distinctly different. When they met, both men were princes (Genesis 36; 32:28), but only one was a prince with God (Genesis 32:28). The greatest difference between these two men was not how terrible they had been, but how much they were forgiven.

Likewise, Jesus forgave the man let down through the roof. Then, to demonstrate the effectiveness of forgiveness, Jesus sent the man home, walking on his own two feet. Luke tells the story by contrasting the healing power of Jesus to forgive the church's administrative delegates who were present but refused His offer (Luke 5:17) with the invalid who welcomed the forgiveness offered (v. 25). By presenting this contrast, it seems Luke wants to highlight the effective, life changing nature of forgiveness as it was experienced by the one man who would accept it.

46 See Luke 23:34 for a particularly strong example.

47 My readers who find themselves helplessly repeating the same action and feeling guilty while they are doing it and afterwards, will be scared by this statement. They, we, want to believe we are forgiven every time we ask for God's forgiveness. We look at our own failings and hope that God will forgive us even though we do not change. These readers have my sympathy, for I have had this experience also. But I cannot bend God to fit my experience. I cannot force Him into my hopes. Experience has taught me two truths. First, the devil loves to make us feel guilty. He is the accuser of every human (Revelation 12:10). The obsession of the devil to accuse us is well documented across the Bible (Job 1:9; 2:4, 5; Zechariah 3:1, 2 provide a few obvious examples). Second, when we repeat the same actions—helplessly doing what we believe to be wrong, it is because we have not really accepted that we are wronging God. No matter how thoroughly we are convinced that our habits are wrong for us, this realization generally does not change us. Only when we accept that we have wronged God and found His forgiveness do we find the power to change our enslaving habits. Judas declared that his actions in betraying Jesus were wrong for himself. "I have sinned in that I have betrayed the innocent blood" (Matthew 27:4). But the Bible never gives the slightest hint that Judas apologized to Jesus nor received forgiveness, even though he admitted his wrongness. His grief drove him to suicide, not to God. In contrast to Judas' confession stands the model confession of all time: David's psalm. David does not focus on his own

wrongness, but on the injustice to God of his own actions. David sees his actions as wronging God. "Against Thee, Thee only, have I sinned" (Psalm 51:4). Judas sees his actions as wrong for himself, but never hints at committing an injustice against the Jesus he knew so well. His silence about mistreating Jesus speaks volumes. David demonstrates a confession that will change us.

The point made in the statement under discussion is that God has not forgiven us when we intentionally repeat our evil actions. If forgiveness only depended on God, we would all be the greatest of saints. He longs to forgive us. But we must accept what He offers before it goes into effect. For too long we have tried to make God into a merciful Being, Who forgives us no matter what we do or say. We want Him to force forgiveness on us while we do nothing to respond. It is true that we cannot earn His favor or His forgiveness; it is equally true that we are not forgiven until we accept His forgiveness.

To those who are haunted by their past, I know Jesus is merciful and tender. He longs to help you. Take a moment to consider how much and how deeply you are hurting Him.

My readers who are theologians are going to scream at this same statement. We have heard so often that Jesus offers forgiveness with no strings attached that we all believe these words. Repetition does not make any lie into truth. What does the Bible actually state about any condition to receive forgiveness?

1. Divine forgiveness is offered to every human being: Romans 2:11; 3:29; 2 Peter 3:9; Galatians 3:26–28; Acts 17:26, 27; John 1:12; 3:16.

2. Divine forgiveness cannot be "bought" with any word or action of the sinner: Ephesians 2:8, 9; John 6:29; Romans 3:28; and many other passages that have already been pointed out by others.

3. Divine forgiveness is forfeited by a human when we refuse to let go of the evil that caused us to need forgiveness: John 3:19, 20; Hosea 4:17; 7:1, 2, 14; 9:17; Ezekiel 18:24, 26, 30–32; Luke 11:24–26; 13:34.

4. Therefore, the previous three points demonstrate that we cannot "shop" for forgiveness, nor offer anything in exchange for it, but we can reject it by clinging to evil. This makes letting go a condition of receiving divine forgiveness.

48   Does God forgive us for doing the same evil action more than once? Yes, but when we fall again, we not only do the wrong itself, but we also disregard His order quoted here to not repeat our mistake. Abraham was forgiven by God (Romans 4:7, 8, 22) for his distrust of God on several occasions. Abraham was brought through the same test in different circumstances until he overcame his own distrust of God. I cannot speak for Abraham specifically, but in my own experience, each time I've had the same test presented to me in different circumstances, I've grown so that when I at last make a clear break with my own past behavior, it is the direct consequence of the little decisions from each time I made the same mistake and realized it.

The experience is similar to a child learning to walk. Children's legs do not learn how to walk instantly. They fall over and over again. But each fall is part of the development of the muscle "memory" that is used over a lifetime of walking. At some point, all of those micro lessons combine into one giant change that we celebrate as a child's first step.

From the outside, we cannot observe all those micro lessons. We simply witness the fruition of their accumulation. Likewise, we cannot judge anyone else as unforgiven because they repeat the same mistake. But we should look introspectively at ourselves.

The problems is that we have people who "never learn to walk," so to speak. They repeat the same mistakes and evils over and over again. Instead of learning micro or macro lessons, they simply excuse or justify themselves, claiming that their own moral behavior is a matter of God's responsibility or the devil's rather than their own. They claim loudly that God forgives them no matter how irresponsibly they behave. These people use a false claim of God's forgiveness to justify bolder and bolder acts of evil.

If we are repeating the same mistake endlessly, it is likely a strong sign that we are being dishonest with ourselves and, more importantly, with God. We are offering excuses that interfere with forgiveness taking place. In my experience, repeating the same mistake is sometimes my first clue that I am deceiving myself with excuses. It is the first revelation that I have not really made things right with God, that my apology to Him was half-hearted. It is the first tangible evidence that I am not reconciled with Him; I am not forgiven.

The woman brought to Jesus in the verse quoted here was guilty of adultery. That was an injustice that Jesus did not excuse (Matthew 5:27, 28). But her behavior quietly communicated what she was not allowed to verbalize under the circumstances—her repentance. She did not try to justify or excuse herself or accuse the men that dragged her there. When Jesus stated that He no longer held her accountable for her contribution to the evil event, He charged her with discontinuing her past actions that contributed to promiscuity. The whole statement constituted His pardon. We cannot uncouple one part from the other for our own convenience.

Some may find Jesus' forgiveness of her unsettling. After all, she was involved in adultery. But the men who brought her were far more powerful. They arguably were guiltier than the woman they accused. When a powerful man rapes a woman (as may have taken place here) and then sanctimoniously covers his disgrace up, our society rightly sees through his hypocrisy. Jesus longed to pardon these men also. Some of these same men may have been present earlier when Luke says "the power of the Lord was present to heal" exactly the kind of men treating this woman so unfairly (Luke 5:17). These men rationalized their own behavior that Jesus exposed (apparently writing it on the sand covered floor) rather than accepting what Jesus offered. Ironically, these men did the woman a favor in bringing her to Jesus and did themselves no favor when they rejected their Savior as they left her alone with Jesus.

But noting the greater moral accountability of these men does not mean the woman was innocent. Jesus stated that He did not condemn her, but that does not mean that He never held her accountable for her wrongdoing. The mercy and forgiveness of Jesus here is not an indication that evil is acceptable but that Jesus is willing to reconcile with those who will let go of their own behavior that they honestly own up to. Jesus does not minimize the enormity of evil but rather maximizes our change from who we were.

49 By abuse here I mean the commission of any act that we know will wrong another person with the expectation that our relationship with that person will not be negatively affected by the act.

50 This seems to be John's point in 1 John 1:8, 10.

51 Readers will no doubt become afraid that I am trying to introduce works and a works-based gospel. Nothing could be further from the truth. The fundamental problem with all works-based theologies is that they teach that some form of human behavior or "works" must precede and "earn" God's forgiveness. I am presenting the opposite: that God's forgiveness, given without human merit, changes human behavior. The results could not be further apart. Attempts to behave "good" to invite or incite God's forgiveness consistently demonstrate the futility of the attempt. The confrontation with God that admits our need of Him and welcomes His grace consistently produces, as Jesus put it: "love" (Luke 7:47).

52 More recently, the Civil Rights Movement in the United States demonstrated the reality of overcoming evil. Discrimination was abandoned by many white Americans when they were exposed to its consequences. We cannot claim that all discrimination was abandoned. But confrontation, education, and legal proscription has changed society at least partially.

This is not to say that the Civil Rights Movement has changed the condition of the human heart. Nor is it to claim that this Movement is the exact equivalent of the process of challenging evil and experiencing forgiveness that I am discussing here, although, in some of its most touching and successful moments, this Movement lived out exactly what I am describing.

But this Movement does prove one thing about evil. Evil is a choice. Discrimination is a choice. Every Anglo Saxon that chooses to sit down in a bus, train, or plane next to an African American demonstrates that refusing to do so in our national past was a choice, not a genetic inevitability.

The Civil Rights Movement has no meaning and no explanation unless it was a way of admitting that we can choose to do or not to do evil. Evil can be overcome, for in many individuals influenced by the Civil Rights Movement, it has been.

We have hardly noticed that the Civil Rights Movement challenges our character on other fronts. If discrimination is an injustice that we can choose to reject when confronted with its true nature, then every other injustice can also be rejected when we are confronted with its true nature.

When Martin Luther King, Jr. famously said, "I have a dream that my four little children will one day live in a nation where they will not be judged by the color of their skin but by the content of their character," (www.archives.gov/press/exhibits/dream-speech.pdf, accessed May 14, 2014) the clear implication was that his children and all children could control their character but not their skin color. Dr. King's speech offers character as a fair criterion for judgment because it is under our control.

We should never miss the underpinnings of the Civil Rights Movement: discrimination and all other forms of injustice are our choice and not just inescapable parts of our DNA; injustice can and should be overcome by making other and better choices; humanity should do all in its power to personally choose justice and influence any other human they can to choose justice.

These philosophical, theological, and metaphysical truths resonate with Jesus' declaration centuries ago: "heaven is here."

53 Noticing that evil and forgiveness are serious matters with God reminds us that God is majestic and powerful and just. These qualities of God are underappreciated today. But let our appreciation of His justice never obscure His mercy. Moses records God's autobiography as including being "merciful," "gracious," and "long-suffering" before it mentions that God "will by no means clear the guilty" (Exodus 34:6, 7). A God who requires us to forgive as often as we are asked to forgive (Matthew 18:21, 22) would not make such a demand if He was unwilling to live by His own rule. God is "not willing that any should perish" (2 Peter 3:9).

54 "Martin Luther King Jr.—Biographical," Nobelprize.org, http://www.nobelprize.org/nobel_prizes/peace/laureates/1964/king-bio.html (accessed February 27, 2014).

55 "Mohandas Gandhi," The History Channel, http://www.history.com/topics/mahatma-gandhi (accessed February 27, 2014).

56 A word of caution against excess is appropriate. Exposing evil is never a good way to "get revenge." A heart of love hides a multitude of evil (paraphrasing 1 Peter 4:8). As with any tool, documenting and exposing evil is a tool that must be used appropriately and never abused. For to abuse this tool is just another act of evil.

57 Matthew 7:3–5. This passage is considered a discussion on judging others. But it teaches as clearly that we ought to be victors over evil and solve our own issues before we offer ourselves to help others. Many problems around us occur because we as a society have found it acceptable to take a course of "helping" others when we are in worse shape than the ones we are trying to help. Instances come to mind of certain sports figures helping boys overcome challenges and be productive citizens while the sport's figure did not control their own sexual urges and therefore added far more challenges to these same boys' lives.

58 It is true that some evils are so terrible that they must be fought by imperfect warriors. Even in our imperfection, the most vulnerable in society deserve whatever we can do to offer them genuine protection. We should never agree with and support evil just because we are not a perfect soldier against all evil.

At the same time, there are evils, as Jesus alluded to in the passage just quoted, that we are unfit to fight because we have greater "issues" at home.

59 "If it feels good" is no justification for doing anything. And at the same time, so far as possible, we should make what is good to do feel good.

60 It has been said that God loves sinners but hates their sin. If we all followed God's example it would create heaven on earth.

61 It is not enough to fight evil and create a vacuum. Daily we need to surrender (see 1 Corinthians 15:31), and then intelligently and diligently apply our minds to fill life with all the goodness of heaven. Christ gave us fair warning about what would happen if we hung on to a little evil in ourselves.

"When the unclean spirit is gone out of a man, he walketh through dry places, seeking rest, and findeth none. Then he saith, I will return into my house from whence I came out; and when he is come, he findeth it empty, swept, and garnished. Then goeth he, and taketh with himself seven other spirits more wicked than himself, and they enter in and dwell there: and the last state of that man is worse than the first. Even so shall it be also unto this wicked generation." (Matthew 12:43–45)

We may happily take in Christ's message, but when we do not daily die to self (see 1 Corinthians 15:31) and completely surrender to the indwelling of the Holy Spirit in our lives, we are resisting Him; thereby, our souls will be destroyed when the demons of our past return full throttle.

62 There is some uncertainty over which eye color went first on that particular day. Mrs. Elliott's methods are also understandably controversial. The controversy does not alter the point of the experiment: we are often unaware of how our words and actions can hurt others who are different from us.

63 Stephen G. Bloom, "Lesson of a Lifetime," Smithsonian.com, September 2005, http://www.smithsonianmag.com/history/lesson-of-a-lifetime-72754306/?page=1 (accessed March 6, 2014).

64 Bruce Watson, "Black Like Me, 50 Years Later," *Smithsonian.com*, http://www.smithsonianmag.com/arts-culture/black-like-me-50-years-later-74543463/?page=1 (accessed March 6, 2014).

65 Martin Luther King, Jr., "I Have a Dream," speech delivered August 28, 1963, http://www.americanrhetoric.com/speeches/mlkihaveadream.htm (accessed March 6, 2013).

66 Today it is argued that merely disagreeing with another person is an act of discrimination. This argument leaves no room for human individuality. It is abusively used to silence intellectual thought and personal conviction. There is no injustice in disagreement. Injustice lies in treating another person condescendingly, rejecting their thoughts for a reason other than the failure of those thoughts' merits, imposing your own personality on the other person against their desire or will, or expecting them to serve you when you are unwilling to reward them properly or serve them in return.

67 "If it be possible, as much as lieth in you, live peaceably with all men" (Romans 12:18). As this passage indicates, we cannot have a healthy relationship with all people. Some will refuse, no matter how decent and respectful we are to them. Not even Jesus had a cordial relationship with all humans. But let us never be the cause of the problem in the relationship. Let us live peaceably, whether others accept our goodwill or not. Let our firmness against evil be manifested in the most decent of ways, so it is clear that we have nothing personal against the one who injures

us. Let us pray with Jesus, "Father, forgive them; for they know not what they do" (Luke 23:34).

68 George Bernard Shaw, Thinkexist.com, http://thinkexist.com/quotation/i_am_ of_the_opinion_that_my_life_belongs_to_the/206708.html (accessed March 6, 2014).

69 Romans 1:14.

70 Heaven never requires us to serve more than we are able. Those who serve too much give themselves hell and defeat the whole point. Let us learn how to protect ourselves without hurting others. Let us learn how to bless and serve others without hurting ourselves.

71 Often, what we can do for others will cost very little to ourselves.

72 M. A. Vroman, publisher, *Sabbath Readings for the Home Circle* (South Lancaster, MA: Couth Lancaster Printing Co., 1905), 251–262.

73 There is no attempt here to change any legal definitions. It is recognized that legal definitions and moral definitions do not always agree, nor should they.

74 See Daniel 10:8, 9.

75 Isaac Newton, "Footprints of the Lion: Isaac Newton at Work," http://www.lib.cam. ac.uk/exhibitions/Footprints_of_the_Lion/introduction.html (accessed March 10, 2014).

76 Dr. Paul Brand & Phillip Yancey, *In His Image* (Grand Rapids, MI: Judith Markham Books, Zondervan Publishing House, 1987), 227-236.

77 Stacia Garland, "Why Children Feel Guilty When Parents Divorce," Exquisite Minds: Gifted and Creative Children, September 21, 2011, http://www.exqui-site-minds.com/idea-of-the-week/why-children-feel-guilty-when-parents-di-vorce/ (accessed March 11, 2014).

78 In distinguishing necessary and unnecessary pain, some mistakenly believe that just to disagree with someone else causes that person pain. These people are always agreeing with those around them, even though their agreeableness leads them to over commitment and other problems that come back to hurt them. This works for a short while, but it is not a long-term success.

When I speak of standing up for ourselves without inflicting unnecessary pain, I mean without injury that may come from our attitudes or from actions meant to get revenge. I never mean that it is to always agree with the other person.

79 "Marie Curie Biography," Bio True Story, A&E Networks, 2014, http://www.biog-raphy.com/people/marie-curie-9263538 (accessed March 12, 2014).

80 "Louis Slotin," Wikipedia: The Free Encyclopedia, http://en.wikipedia.org/wiki/ Louis_Slotin (accessed March 12, 2014).

81 Clifford T. Honicker, "America's Radiation Victims: The Hidden Files," *New York Times*, November 19, 1989, http://www.nytimes.com/1989/11/19/magazine/amer ica-s-radiation-victims-the-hidden-files.html